The Action Taker's
Real Estate Investing Planner

By **QUENTIN D'SOUZA**

The Action Taker's Real Estate Investing Planner

Publisher: DREIC Publishing

Copyright Canada, USA & the World 2020

Feedback and Comments: info@actiontakerrealestateplanner.com

ISBN: 978-0-9936717-3-9

The Action Taker's
Real Estate
Investing Planner

By QUENTIN D'SOUZA

DREIC Publishing 2020

4

Acknowledgements

I started writing this planner at an EO (Entrepreneurs Organization) event in July 2019. I have always been someone that has been driven to achieve goals, and push others to do the same. I feel that EO and in particular my Forum has helped me enormously over the years in this capacity and in many other. I would encourage you, as I mention in this book to find peers as good as these men and women.

Beginning in 2014, I started using and revising templates that you will find in this planner with hundreds of coaching clients. They have allowed me to fine tune these templates in order for them to be more functional for a broader audience. There would be so many to thank, and without naming you all personally, I would like to thank you.

I want to thank DurhamREI members and EducationREI members for giving me feedback on the numerous handouts and video training that I produce for members. It is with this feedback that I have been able to fine tune the content in this planner.

For a number of years I worked with a business coach named Andrew Barber-Starkey, Founder and President of The ProCoach System. I would travel to British Columbia for planning sessions. He introduced me to quarterly and weekly planning and some of the tools and templates come directly from those experiences with him, repurposed for real estate investors. I would encourage anyone to look him up and work with him, especially if you are working with a coach for the first time.

More recently, I have been in the Strategic Coach Program with Dan Sullivan, and have been able to take advantage of the many tools that have been made able to help me. They have helped to shift my mindset and help me to work on a number of entrepreneurial skills. I can't say enough about the amazing people that make up "Coach" and everything about the program. Again, I would encourage you to work with them.

I'd like to thank my wife Laura, for listening to me talk real estate in the evening, on weekends and every other time when she would rather not hear about a tenant, deal, house or apartment building. Her support means the world to me.

Finally, I wanted to encourage my two sons – Darcy and Lucas to use this planner to help them to achieve their financial goals, but also any other goals that they want to achieve. If you can dream it, you can achieve it. All you need to do is shift your mindset, and everything else will follow.

Table of Contents

Chapter 3: Your Quarterly Plan — 47

Chapter 4: Your Weekly Plan — 59

CHAPTER 1

Why Real Estate Investors Fail and Why Traditional Goal Setting Doesn't Work, Roadblocks and Detours

THE SIDE HUSTLE THAT FIZZLES OUT - THE MAJOR CHALLENGES TO YOUR REAL ESTATE SUCCESS

"Most people underestimate what they can do in ten or twenty years and overestimate what they can do in one year." ~ Tony Robbins

Does Planning Actually Work?

Research conducted by the University of Scranton revealed that 77% of people who committed to a New Year's resolution stuck to it for at least a week. That same study indicated that only 8% of people who made that same resolution actually completed that goal in a timely manner or if ever.[1]

Why Traditional Goal Setting Doesn't Work, Roadblocks and Detours

What is happening with goal setting and why it is not working, and what you can do about it?

Typically, in the first few days of January, you will get asked by a family member or friend about your goals for the following year. You might come up with a health-related goal like losing weight or eating better. In the first week or two after you have made the goal, everything is going great and you feel like you are making inroads.

Then something happens, you are distracted and think that okay I'll just do this or eat this just one time. Then the next time you make the same excuse, finally you are back in the same position and in the same routines as you were before.

Has this ever happened to you when you have been setting a goal for yourself?

Now it's time to try something different.

Albert Einstein is widely credited with saying, "The definition of insanity is doing the same thing over and over again, but expecting different results."

If you have been doing the same thing over and over again, you are most likely getting the same results. If you picked up this book, I am going to push you to do something different, in order to get different results.

Over the last year, I have lost over 100 pounds, run a marathon, and added $5 million of assets (27 units) to my real estate portfolio. I am not special. I believe that anybody can do what I have done. They just need to follow a few systems and processes that we will go through in this journal.

---

1   **"The resolution solution: longitudinal examination of New Year's change attempts." University of Scranton,** https://www.ncbi.nlm.nih.gov/pubmed/2980864

The Major Challenges to Your Real Estate Success

What Are You Saying to Yourself?

One thing that I am very careful about is the language that I am using, particularly, when I'm describing the actions that I am trying to achieve. When I reflect about the times when I used sarcasm or was self-effacing I would often blow it off. But it actually affected my confidence of what I was trying to achieve. Your words, whether out loud or in your head, are important. What you tell yourself and what your inner voice says makes a difference. The language that you use helps to shape who you are.

One example is using the word "try."

I have heard too many real estate investors say that they are going to "try" something only to give up when things get a little hard. Just remember, if it were easy everyone would do it.

The only thing that you should be trying is new foods or a new drink. But you don't try to lose weight and you don't try to buy rental property. That is a recipe for failure. Set the goal with a strong "I will" statement in order to set the tone for success.

Your Mindset and Your Net Worth

If you are constantly complaining about other people, things, or blame events that happen to you that are out of your control, you are giving power to someone else or something else. The truth is that you are in control of your life. It is only you that can change your mindset.

When I first started investing in real estate, I thought that mindset was some foo-foo thing. But I realized that as I grew my portfolio, my limiting beliefs were things that I had grown up with. The only way to change what I was doing was to change my mindset.

I realized very quickly that whatever you focus on grows. Whether that is your net worth or the amount of pounds that you've lost. The more that you focus on that particular area of your life, the more you will see improvement in it.

To take this a step further, when you measure what you focus on, it grows even further and faster. I suggest that you track your net worth by completing a simple balance sheet each time you work on your goals.

It helps to establish where you are and helps you to get where you want to go.

Here is an example of a simple balance sheet that you can update each quarter in order to help you to focus on this goal. It lumps everything together so that you can quickly come up with a net worth amount.

BALANCE SHEET			
ASSETS		**LIABILITIES**	
Total Deposits:		Unsecured LOC:	
Unregistered Investments:		Car and Personal Loans:	
Registered Investments:		Secured Lines of Credit:	
Real Estate Portfolio:		Mortgages:	
Personal Assets:		Other:	
Other:			
Total Assets		Total Liabilities:	
Total Assets -Total Liabilities = **Net Worth:**			

☐ **High Net Worth Canadians**($1M-$5M) ☐ **Mid-Tier Millionaires**($5M-$30M) ☐ **Ultra High Net Worth**($30M+)

There was a great report from Capgemini/RBC Wealth Management, the "2015 World Wealth Report," which breaks down "rich" into three categories, which may help you to define your goals. There are a few numbers that may give you some perspective.

	High Net Worth	**Mid-Tier Millionaires**	**Ultra-High Net Worth**
Investable Assets (Not Including Primary Residence)	US $1 million to US$5 million	US$5 million to US$30 million	US$30 million+
Number of Canadians	298,000	30,000	3,300
Percentage of the Population	Less than 1%	Less than 0.1%	Less than 0.01%

These are again simple targets to help you to achieve your financial goals. It does not mean that the goals are easy but that you have a specific number for you to strive for.

Get Out of Your Comfort Zone

I've heard the statement "Get out of your comfort zone" dozens of times over the years. It was not until I quantified how it made me feel that allowed me to understand what it means. For me, "Getting Out Of Your Comfort Zone" often includes a physical reaction.

Usually, I have a feeling in my stomach almost like a roller coaster that tells me I'm doing something that I have never really done before.

For you, the feeling might be a little different, but whatever that feeling is, it's doing something which is different from what you have ever done before.

Once I have done the particular task, I am more comfortable doing it again and again. Then it is no longer outside of my comfort zone.

Buying my first rental property was exactly that. I was nervous asking dozens of questions and I'm sure the real estate agent that was helping me was tired of answering all of my questions. Once we had purchased a property, I think she avoided taking my phone calls for a little while to take a break.

Once the first property was purchased, it was much easier to purchase the second and third property. I knew what to expect but there were definitely variables that I wasn't expecting. The second property that I purchased was a private sale. The third property that I purchased was a freehold townhouse, where I had lost the property initially to a multiple offer situation. But then the winning offer dropped away and I became the only offer and was able to close on the property. The seller also requested a closing date that was six months after the purchase and sale agreement was signed.

The big uncomfortable first purchase helped to lead me to financial freedom and the ability to work for myself and create a business where I no longer have to give my time hourly to anybody else.

You never know what you'll be able to do if you get out of your comfort zone—until you do it.

When Should You Review Your Goals?

My answer to this question is—"Often."

What many people do is write down their goals at the beginning of the year. They will create a list of things that they want to get done.

Maybe they put it on their cell phone.

Maybe they made out a list.

Then they put it somewhere that they never look at again, until December rolls around and they're thinking about the goals that they set at the beginning of the year. And how they weren't able to complete them.

Whenever you set goals for yourself you should place them in an area that you can see every day. I am a big advocate of having your goals posted publicly, written beside your desk or a place where you can read it whenever you are doing any sort of planning. You will start to see how this can really work to your benefit when you do a weekly plan.

I am not an advocate of annual goals. I believe that those goals are too far away for you to be able to achieve within a reasonable amount of time. I feel that unless the goal is based on a quarter year (twelve-week) time frame, they will be easily forgotten. Sometimes the season affects the type of goals that you have. The goals that you have during the summer may be different than the goals that you have during the winter.

For example, once I set my desired outcome was losing a hundred pounds, I was actually stating quarterly goals of losing twenty-five pounds each quarter. That was my desired outcome for the twelve weeks. I then would attach three actions that helped me to obtain that goal. One action was walking every day, another action to eliminate snacking after 9:00 p.m., then a third action was to join a group of like-minded people who were also losing weight.

The desired outcome and the three actions were posted beside my desk. And I reviewed them every time I made plans for the week. I included these goals in my schedule. I focused on them and decided that I needed to wake up earlier than everybody else in order to achieve them. So I began waking up an hour before any of my other family members in order to get my walk done. I made time, I didn't make excuses.

Don't Give Up (Forgive Yourself)

Did I always do what I had planned to do? The answer is no. There were many times that I failed. I ate the wrong foods that I knew weren't going to help me to lose that weight. In my real estate business, I began using a rent-to-own strategy that created income but never really created wealth.

The one thing that I have learned, is that you need to forgive yourself. You need to be able to say, I recognize that this was a mistake and I don't want to make that mistake again. I am starting from day one again. I start the process as if it were the first time I have been doing the activity. If I ate a meal that took me in the wrong direction, I would start again eating well. With real estate investing, it was making sure to analyze my entrance and exit strategies that they are aligned with my big why.

Know Your Big Why

Why are you investing in real estate? Is it to create income or are there bigger reasons for investing in real estate. Often, you have to dig down five layers to figure out your big why. This technique is called "The 5 Whys." It was originally developed by Sakichi Toyoda, the Japanese industrialist, inventor, and founder of Toyota Industries, in the 1930s.

When applied to your reasons for investing in real estate, it might go something like the below example. This is where I went down four **WHYS** in order to get to an answer that was more profound to me.

Why One: Why was I investing in real estate? At first, I thought it was because I was interested in creating income to be able to leave my job.

Why Two: Then I asked myself why did I want to leave my job? Well, I wanted to have more time and control over my time. Having the finances allowed me to create my own schedule.

Why Three: The next question was why did I want to create my own schedule?. Because there were a number of things that I wanted to do with my life other than work. I wanted to write books so that I can help people to achieve their own goals. I wanted to spend time with my kids and take them to school or events or just to experience life.

Why Four: Why did I want to do that? Because I wanted to be a good father and a good husband and a good person.

I knew I could do all of those things without having to use real estate. But I also knew that real estate would help me to do those things and in the long run be better off. Knowing your why is an important step. But it's more than looking at the goal that you sell it for yourself. It's really about looking much deeper than that. You've got to go down three or four levels in order to find the **BIG WHY** and reasoning behind what you are doing.

Your Environment Affects Your Success

The environment that you are in will affect your success. It can help or hinder what you endeavor to do. Your determination can push through but it is so much easier if you can set yourself up for success.

For example, if you are writing a book, you need to remove the distractions like your cell phone or internet access in order to keep focused on getting your writing done. This will become a natural part of the process when you are writing. And to help you succeed, the same thing can be done for whatever goal you set out to do.

For real estate investing, you will want to have books that you can refer to, and you will want to have an environmental space that will allow you to focus on building your real estate business. This might be an office or a nook in your home. You might have books that end up with writing in them from your notes and a growing collection of course material binders. Some of the wealthiest people I know are very proud of their library, you should be too.

Also, with real estate investing, this usually means removing distractions from your life—maybe it means canceling that Netflix account or removing television from the house. Whatever it is that distracts you may require you to take drastic actions by eliminating it from your area or your schedule.

Use time tracking to identify exactly what you are doing each hour of the day for a week. This tool will help you to examine what environmental things are happening that are distracting you from your goals.

Time	Monday
5:00-6:00 AM	
6:00-7:00 AM	
6:00-7:00 AM	Wake up/Breakfast/Workout
7:00-8:00 AM	Kids Off to School
8:00-9:00 AM	Travel to Work
9:00-10:00 AM	Work
10:00-11:00 AM	Work
11:00-12:00 PM	Work
12:00-1:00 PM	Lunch and Audiobook
1:00-2:00 PM	Work
2:00-3:00 PM	Work
3:00-4:00 PM	Work
4:00-5:00 PM	Work
5:00-6:00 PM	Travel Home
6:00-7:00 PM	Dinner
7:00-8:00 PM	Kids Hockey Game
8:00-9:00 PM	Family Time/Goodnight to Kids
9:00-10:00 PM	Private Seller Leads Followup
10:00-11:00 PM	Review Private Seller Course Materials
11:00-12:00 AM	Sleep

If you are trying to lose weight, it makes no sense for other family members to have bags of cookies and chips all around you. It makes it more difficult for you in order to achieve your goals and your loved ones who support you should be able to come up with some alternatives or create something that's hidden from you so that they can enjoy their snacks but you will never be able to see it or know where it comes from.

If you are trying to do more running, it's important that you have the correct running shoes that would allow you to run in your daily field of vision. Particularly, having the right equipment near you helps to remind you that you should be out there going for a run.

The essence of this concept is that you are creating an environment that supports whatever goal that you are trying to achieve.

What Are You Feeding Your Mind?

As a real estate investor, you are constantly learning new things and applying them to your business. You must continue to do this every day, whether this is reading a book, white papers, or specific investor focused reports. If you are constantly watching the media, who write headlines that grab your attention, you will diverge from what is really important—your goals. Whether you are paying attention to politics or not, if you don't have your own life running the way that you wanted, how do you expect to make change in other places? Focus on learning and growing yourself, whether that is in real estate knowledge or personal development.

An easy way to do that now is through podcasts. There are a number of podcasts that are out there that continue to improve over time. I am reluctant to recommend a few just because they come and go over time. But the best thing that you could do is do a search for Canadian Real Estate Investing and see which podcasts come up in your favorite pod catcher.

When you have transition time, make sure that you use it. This is a great time to be listening to podcasts. The key I find with listening to podcasts is to write down one action that comes from the podcast. It makes it easier for you to pull something from that if you write down one thing that you learned. If you find that you have nothing to write down after listening to a podcast, it is probably time to unsubscribe from it.

Another way that you can listen to great materials is through audiobooks. I have an Audible account as well as an Audiobooks account. They are both excellent resources for purchasing books that you can listen to. Again, the key with books is to write down actionable items. I focus on picking three big topics that come from every book that I read and see how that might apply or not apply in some cases to my business. The idea here is that you are constantly growing from what you are learning.

The challenge in this day and age is not the availability of the information that you can find but the ability to act on those pieces of information. There is so much available and so much information that you can learn from. The key is actually internalizing it, completing an action, and doing something with it.

Personal Development

What will you learn this quarter?

☐ Crushing It in Apartment
Buildings Book

☐ Secret Life of Real Estate and
Banking Book

☐ Definitive Guide to Underwriting
Multifamily Acquisitions Book

Attending Masterminds and Groups

While you are growing your real estate portfolio, people will always question your intentions. They will ask you questions like, isn't it risky to invest in real estate, how much is enough, or why don't you just hand over your money to a financial planner. You should have an answer ready. The one that has worked for me is telling people that I have a gift and the gift is to create wealth in real estate. Just like crabs in a bucket, people will often pull you down to where they are.

There is a crab mentality amongst people. It is a way of thinking best described by the phrase, "If I can't have it, neither can you." It is a pattern of behavior noted in crabs when they are trapped in a bucket. While any one crab could easily escape, its efforts will be undermined by others, ensuring the group's collective demise. The analogy in human behavior is claimed to be that members of a group will attempt to reduce the self-confidence of any member who achieves success beyond the others out of envy, resentment, spite, conspiracy, or competitive feelings to halt their progress.

Another way to feed your mind with positive information is through lunch meetings or masterminds with people who do not have the crab mentality. I find that I can meet with at least one person a week for lunch and develop them as a center of influence. If I find that they are going to have a positive impact on my life, I will make a habit of meeting with them for lunch more often. Others that I meet, I meet only once and may never meet with them again because I find that they are not a positive influence in my life.

The other way that I do this is through joining mastermind groups. I have formed mastermind groups in the past and grown out of mastermind groups. The point is that we are able to learn from the people around us and it's especially useful if you're growing in the same direction. The challenge always occurs when some people are growing in a particular direction similar to you and others are retreating back into a different phase of life. That is often an indication for you to move from one mastermind group into another.

Here are some questions to ask in order to help you to find a great group:

1. Who is leading the Group? Are they an expert in the area that you want to learn?

2. What is the Group's business model? Are they earning a commission on sales, is there a monthly fee or both? If there is a monthly fee, what do you get for that fee?

3. What is the Experience Level of the group? There should be people attending that are at your level, below your level, and above your level in the group.

4. All good groups have Process and Procedure Rules in order to not waste anyone's time. What are the Rules for Participating in the Group?

5. When do they meet and are you available to attend? In person meetings are great for developing relationships with people, online meetings are useful for content delivery but not necessarily good for developing relationships.

6. What are some skills that you can bring to the Group? How can I add value to the Group?

There are a few groups that you can join where I would recommend as a great resource to find like-minded people, but often there are specific criteria in order to access these groups. The Entrepreneurs Organization is a great place for meeting other entrepreneurs, who are moving in the same direction as you. EO is a not for profit organization worldwide. I find that this group of people are very active in their businesses and are on the growth phase of building their business.

Tiger 21 is another group that I would highly recommend with a high threshold for attendance. The group is for people who are at a later stage of their real estate investing or life. Where they are defending the wealth that these business owners and entrepreneurs have already grown over the years. This is a great group of people that can help you to grow and learn.

There are other groups out there that are very similar to these two groups, but you should do your own due diligence on whether you will find these groups helpful. Both of the above groups have a high threshold participation. It can make it a challenge for people to join but it also means that you have higher-quality people in the different groups.

Sometimes it's important to be able to get information from people who are not in the same business as you in order to cross pollinate your ideas with the ideas from other businesses. This helps you to innovate what you're doing and helps you to grow your business differently than other people. Often, you hear of companies that have been able to innovate based on their connection with another business.

There are many groups online where you can meet up with other people who are interested in real estate investing. A perfect example of this is meetup.com. It's a great place for you to search out other like-minded people who are learning. You can search for the topic of real estate in your area. And you can join a group of people. Just make sure that the people that you are meeting with are actually buying real estate. I often find that in these groups 80 percent of people are learning and 20 percent of people are doing. What you should be looking for is a demographic where 80 percent of the people are doing and 20 percent of the people are learning. That gives you a strong knowledge base to draw upon. If you don't have a group nearby, meetup.com makes it easy for you to create your own group. I've often talked to people who started off with just a few people and have grown over time to twenty to fifty people that were meeting monthly to help each other and help their business grow.

Facebook groups are another example of like-minded people getting together and sharing their goals, interests, and sometimes even leads with each other. If you can find a good Facebook group that's active and that's not just promoting a particular business, course, or event, it can be a great place for you to help each other and network as well as get questions answered quickly. My only caveat when it comes to Facebook groups is there are lots of opinions and it doesn't mean that they're legal, ethical, or a great way of approaching things from a business perspective. Whenever you get any sort of advice from a Facebook group or person online, make sure that you know who that person is that you're getting that advice from, otherwise you might as well have picked up that piece of advice from the street corner. That is not the way to build a business or get advice. You pay professionals to help you to get things done professionally, not what you might find on a street corner.

Roadblocks for Real Estate Investors

Over the last twelve years, I have met with thousands of real estate investors. There are three major roadblocks that every real estate investor who is successful comes across. How they deal with these roadblocks will often indicate to me whether they will be successful or whether they will stop real estate investing.

The Three Real Estate Investing Roadblocks Are: Financing, Funding, and Finding

Eventually, every real estate investor comes to a point where they are challenged with being able to finance real estate investment. For some people, this might be something that happens right out of the gate. So their first property is one where they have a challenge financing it. For other people, it may be the fifth property or the tenth property or the twentieth property. Whatever it is, financing will often become a challenge at one time or another. How investors deal with that challenge often indicates whether they will continue to grow or not.

When running up to this challenge, some investors will talk to one banker and if they are told no **they will give up**. Other investors will talk to three bankers and if they are not able to get a mortgage **they will give up.** Still other in-depth investors will talk to five banks and if they are not able to get a mortgage **they will give up**. Some investors will talk to five banks and three mortgage brokers, they will start to work with the lenders, they will talk to credit unions. Then if they are not able to get a mortgage, **they will give up**. Other investors will do all of the same as the last group, then they will talk to potential partners; those partners will act as mortgage qualifiers and help them to be able to qualify for a mortgage. And their ability to be able to grow continues. How determined are you to be able to get your financing done? You cannot accept no as an answer. You must continue to be determined. If not, you may want to partner with somebody else who is more determined than you.

I have this on my desk:

Eventually everybody runs out of money who invests in real estate.

This is the truth when it comes to real estate investing. It could be that this happens when you are investing with your first property and you just don't have the funds to be able to purchase it but you have the expertise and the qualification.

For other people, this could be their third, fourth, or fifth property where they run out of funds. If this is something that happens to you, what are you going to do about it? Are you going to talk to different banks in order to get access to lines of credit and see if you can utilize those as part of your lending strategy? Did you arrange your financing so that you included home equity lines of credit so that as you pay down your properties you would access equity or mortgage, pay down as a line of credit so that is a secured line of credit so that you could use that to purchase more property? Have you decided to approach partners and have them bring the down payment and you manage and find the properties and act as the property expert? If that is the case, it is very possible that you will have unlimited growth. You need to decide whether this last approach is for you and that you are determined to be able to do this.

From even the most experienced investor's I have heard, "I can't find a good deal anywhere." There are a number of different things that you need to work through when it comes to finding properties but there is always a challenge of where you're looking for properties. This will always affect your ability to find good properties.

If you are looking where everybody else is looking, such as the MLS, you are going to be competing with everybody else in order to purchase those properties. If you are willing to do what other people aren't willing to do, which is advertise or talk to people about properties that may not be listed on the MLS, then you are more likely to find opportunities that are coming about. I have often found that there are two ways to find great deals. You can either negotiate them or you can create them.

By negotiating a great deal, this could be through finding how you can help solve a problem that the seller has and in order to help them solve that problem you are going to be able to get a lower price on the purchase of the house. This could mean closing the property in two weeks or allowing a seller to stay in the property for a few months after the close. Whatever your solution is, it helps the seller to solve a problem and will allow you to negotiate a great deal.

The other way for you to find a great deal is to create one—usually it means bringing a property into its highest and best use. That is when you look at a property and see what other people don't see. Maybe that is looking at a house that has an extra lot beside it, severing that lot, selling it off, and then keeping the house. That is taking a deal and being creative about it in order to come up with something new. That could be taking a detached house and adding an accessory apartment to it in order to create additional value. Whatever that is, you need to be more creative than the other people who were looking at the same property.

Every real estate investor needs to be able to focus on these three areas. Finding, funding, and financing deals. You need to be able to include them in your quarterly plans, as well as your weekly plans, if you want to continue to build your real estate business. That's why this *Real Estate Entrepreneur's Journal* helps to focus on these areas.

Consistent growth in these three areas helps your real estate portfolio grow:		
Finding	**Funding**	**Financing**
☐ Get 10-20+ Unit building under contract ☐ 10 New lead sources in apartment building	☐ 2 New JV Partners with 500k+ to invest ☐ Have 1 million in Accessible Cash/Credit	☐ Complete Refi of USA Portfolio with Morgan ☐ Prepare Financing Binder for Apps

The Real Estate Solopreneur Trap - Reason for Doing, Delegating, and Dumping

There is a trap that happens when you are developing a business that is the trap of becoming a **Solopreneur**. Really what that means is that you have created a job for yourself. A solopreneur is somebody who has basically created a job for themselves through their real estate purchases. Their real estate investments help to pay them each month but they need to continue to work at it every day in order for it to be successful.

The difference is people who create a real estate business. They have bookkeepers, property managers, and others who helped them to do the day-to-day work of their business. Those are people who have created a business and not a job for themselves. It allows them to travel and to do other things. If you are in the solopreneur trap, you are always on call for your properties. You are doing all the accounting and bookkeeping for your properties. You are the one that is going out to properties to try to identify whether there is a repair necessary or not. Those are some examples of a solopreneur in real estate. If you are one of them, then you need to use this journal to help you to create processes and systems every week to remove yourself from the day-to-day grind.

These processes and systems are what you will pass on to other people. You can take time to train them and then they can follow through on that process and system. If they aren't doing a good job, you can hire somebody else to do that same job. This requires you to get out of your comfort zone and do something that you have perhaps never done before, if you have never run a business before.

It is easy to create a job and be self-employed using real estate. It's much more challenging to create a business around it.

Some parts of real estate are more naturally an active real estate business. House flipping is a good example of people who are creating a job for themselves. Especially if they do not have a team of people around them. HGTV has created a mentality that the process is just so simple. Buy it for $500,000, put $200,000 into it, and sell it for $1 million, while it doesn't really work like that in real life. So you need to figure out how you can create the systems and processes in your business and then hand those systems and processes to other people. Make sure that you are writing these at least once a week or improving the systems that you already have so that you can continue to hand these out to other people.

One of the things that we are going to be focusing on in this journal is your ability to either get a task done, delegate it by passing it off to somebody else, or stop doing that task altogether.

When you are doing something actively in your business, you need to decide whether this is something that you should be doing all the time. For example, perhaps you have a form that is being filled out for each property. Maybe for insurance purposes you need to get that form filled out. Now you are buying four or five properties a year and you are able to get a lot of this information from the listing. Why not have your realtor send the listing to a virtual assistant who can complete the form for you. You can review it, make any changes, and send it off. It would be better if you have your virtual assistant send that form to somebody else in your business, perhaps a local assistant to review it and then move on with the form process. Then send it off to your insurance person. Whatever that is, you need to come up with the ability for you to either do it, delegate it, or dump it. That is the way that you can scale and grow your system, often delegating means creating processes and systems.

Delegate

What task(s) will you delegate this quarter?

☐ Assistant to do Utilities Processing

☐ Assistant to do monthly Insurance Checklist

Sources of Income

Some of the big tools that have helped me tremendously are often simple visualizations. Here is a perfect example with the sources of income that you have per month.

Sources of Income per Month

1. Salary/Hourly	$_____
2. Monthly Cash Flow After Expenses	$_____
3. Business Profits	$_____
4. Residuals	$_____
5. Interest Income	$_____
6. Pensions, Benefits	$_____
7. Dividend Earnings	$_____
8. Sale of Assets	$_____
TOTAL	$_____

I have used this tool and would ask that you update this quarterly. This will give you a great example of where you are from an income perspective and where you want to go. It also gives you the opportunity to see what would happen if you were to lose one source of your income. Let's say you were a T4 employee that lost their job. Perhaps, you are laid off or there was some downsizing. Now that you can cross off that income source what happens to you? Do you need to go on unemployment insurance in order to survive?

If you are a real estate investor, then you would use one of your other sources of income to be able to do this. You might use the cash flow that comes from the business. Your real estate assets will throw off income after all expenses are paid. That income is something that you might be able to use as long as you have purchased your property correctly.

If you have separate business outside of real estate or maybe related to real estate, that income is something that you can use. Instead of plowing the money back into your business, you may be able to take advantage of using the income for yourself.

Perhaps, you have intellectual property that you have created and published. This could be a paper book, audiobook, or e-book that you have made available and continues to sell. Perhaps, you're making a couple hundred dollars a month from that.

Maybe you are lending money from funds that you have created in your business. Perhaps, you are lending money at 8 percent and borrowing money at 4 percent and you're able to keep the difference. Or you sold assets and are now collecting income from those assets by lending first mortgages or second mortgages.

Maybe you are purchasing dividend bearing stocks that create income every month. Maybe these are blue-chip stocks that have been and are dividend aristocrats stocks that have been paying dividends for twenty years or more. The ability of those stocks to continue to give dividends is a benefit to you and something that you may want to include as your income.

Maybe you're more of an active stock investor and do option trading as a method to generate additional income for your stock portfolio. By using an active strategy, you create an additional income source for yourself.

Perhaps, you are selling off some of your assets to generate cash for yourself. Or maybe instead of selling an asset, you refinance an asset in order to pull money out of that asset, either to create income for yourself or invest in purchasing another asset.

You can see that through real estate and also through the stock market you can create different income sources. The challenge I gave to you is to be able to cross off one or two of these income sources and see if you are still able to generate the monthly income that you want. If you can do that, you've created enough flexibility in your income sources in order to withstand different stresses.

Making Money and Keeping Money Strategy

We Want Stores of Real Value to Own

I am a big believer in owning hard assets. Over the last hundred years, we have had a consistent asset inflation rate that has increased the value of hard assets. Those who do not own hard assets will always work for those who do.

It is a well-known fact that most Canadians have a majority of net worth in their personal residence, not from savings or investments in the stock market. Those people who own more homes have more net worth than others. I know more multimillionaires who have made their money through real estate than in any other business. I may be a little biased though. Whatever you do, whenever you buy a real asset, you add real value to your net worth.

Whether it is houses, multifamily buildings, commercial buildings, or industrial buildings, they all appreciate over time due to asset inflation, increases of the money supply, and supply/demand.

Land is another example of a hard asset, although it does not produce income unless you are farming it, but it retains value because they are not making any more of it. Because of this, there is a limited supply issue. In some areas, there is a higher demand because there are more people who will live in a particular area and that's pushing up the value of the land. Well-positioned land has done well for people over generations. The challenge, of course, is holding on to land over time when you are not producing any income from it.

Investing in profitable businesses could mean direct private investment in a business. This is often referred to as a partnership. This could be somebody investing directly in private equity or this could be investment in a blue-chip stock on the stock market. There are benefits to investing in profitable businesses.

Another type of hard asset that is often missed is intellectual property. Either creating your own books, songs, music, audiobooks, whatever it may be, owning intellectual property that can be a source of income for you. Some artists even fell with their intellectual property in order to create money now in order to create an income stream for somebody else in the future. Although these assets are often more soft than hard, they are still assets and that I would consider part of the portfolio.

Oftentimes, I will talk about intellectual property as an asset. I consider it an asset because you can collect a stream of income from it. In order to create intellectual property, the production requires a lot of time and effort. This could be a book, song, or invention where we collect royalties on a particular product. These royalties are a stream of income that you can collect on a monthly basis for as long as you own the intellectual property rights.

There are new services that are coming out which allow you to take advantage of somebody else's existing intellectual property and purchase a stream of income by giving a fixed payment upfront.

One such service is called royalty exchange, www.royaltyexchange.com, where you have an auction style purchase process. On this site, you are able to purchase a portion or percentage of a musician, songwriter, producer, or artist's royalties. This allows artists to leverage their existing music catalog to raise money to fund other projects.

Some of the artists that you see here spanned from music in television shows—Beyoncé, Kylie Minogue, Drake, Santana, and the Grateful Dead.

Another such service is called www.songvest.com, which seems to be a lot newer to the same space. Perhaps, you can add this new stream of income through purchasing intellectual property assets of your favorite songs to your financial freedom formula.

Another source of hard assets are gold/silver/jewelry/artwork.

These are all asset types that maintain their value or increase in value over time based on supply and demand. There is only one *Mona Lisa*. If you were to have owned that painting over time you would have gained more value than if you owned another type of painting. The idea is that you own these types of assets. Similar to song royalties, there are new services like www.masterworks.io, which helps you to buy fractional ownership of art works of well-known artists.

Precious metals can be easily accessible to you through the purchase of gold and silver. The key to owning that type of asset though is to make sure to store it off-site in a place that makes sense to you and that you are able to easily access. I do not recommend storing them in a bank deposit box but there are other places that you can store them. I don't recommend storing this at your home at all.

One thing that I have above my desk is a reminder to purchase hard assets. I have a picture of a one trillion bill that's from the reserve Bank of Zimbabwe. And the other is a one quadrillion dollar bill and that is from Hungary. It's a good example of why you want to have a hard asset versus paper money in a bank account.

Unless we have the severe deflationary environment, all currencies go down in value over time. It is a supply and demand issue. Countries through their central banks control their dollar printing presses that are constantly being pushed into the economy. It is a simplistic way of viewing inflation but if there were less dollars printed they would be worth more. The challenge we have is making sure that we are liquid enough to be able to use dollars to purchase hard assets when they are on sale or when we believe that we can negotiate or create a great deal.

CHAPTER 2

The Real Estate Entrepreneurs Planning Process

THE SECRET SAUCE TO YOUR SUCCESS

"If you don't design your own life plan, chances are you'll fall into someone else's plan. And guess what they have planned for you? Not much." ~ Jim Rohn

In order to succeed in building a successful real estate business, you need to think big. But you also need to be laser focused on tasks that need to get done each week.

This journal will help you to focus on both your big picture, as well as those weekly tasks that you need to get done in order for you to be able to succeed.

Work on Your Big Rocks

There is a story about a professor who picked up a large empty last glass jar and showed it to his class. The professor begins filling the jar to the top with rocks that are three to four inches in diameter. He then asked the class if the jar is full and they proceeded to say yes. Then the professor takes a bowl of pebbles and puts them in the jar. He shakes the jar and the pebbles settle in between the spaces between the big rocks. He asks the class again if the jar was full and the class responds yes. Finally, the professor pulls out a bag of sand and he pours it into the jar until the space between the sand fills the rocks and pebbles. Then the professor takes a bottle of water and pours it into the jar. It reaches the materials inside and then settles into the sand until there is no more room in the jar. He then states now this jar is full.

He asks the class that if the sand and water were put into the jar first, would there have been enough room for the big rocks and pebbles as well?

The moral of the story is quite simple and directly relates to what we are doing here.

The big rocks are your long-term goals. These are your ten- to twenty-year goals that help to provide direction in what you are doing. The pebbles are your shorter-term quarterly goals. The sand is your weekly goals that help to fill your week and the water is the distractions that happen and prevent you from getting work done.

If you take the time to identify what your big rocks are, the pebbles and sand will more easily fall in place and you won't get distracted by the water and lose sight of your objectives. Remember, it is not about having a huge number of items on the list but rather a progression towards your long-term goals.

Before You Think Big - Think About This

Do you have a middle-class or a wealthy mindset?

There is a great book that I recommend people read, it is titled *The Top 10 Distinctions Between Millionaires and the Middle Class* by Keith Cameron Smith. This is a great big picture mindset book, and I wanted to highlight a few things that inspired me around this topic.

The middle-class mindset plans. Often, the plans are related to saving and hoping for something for the future. They are taxed the highest because of how they earn their income and continue to be so throughout their lives. Their plans are often controlled by other people, either financial planners, government, pensions, or other institutions. They are told, or rather sold, a particular net worth goal.

The wealthy mindset strategizes. They create assets that pay them every single month. They work their team to help them get taxed efficiently, not only annually but throughout their lifetime. The wealthy control their own wealth. They focus on cash flow within their strategy.

The middle-class mindset focuses on products they are sold RRSPs, EPS, stocks, gold, single family homes to live in, specific stocks, mutual funds, and bonds. Many have a goal of a pension.

The wealthy mindset strategizes. They consider different risks whether political, taxes, economic changes, consider hedging. They maximize their returns by looking at the interconnectedness of strategy.

The middle class are sold the concept of diversification. They invest mainly in their primary residence, mutual funds, stocks, and bonds. They have very little control over their results.

The wealthy focus on investing directly into one asset or business. They gain expertise in that area to a point where they are doing well. They understand that they can control assets and manipulate their returns through the control of those assets. Once they have an expert understanding of the asset, they expand into other areas.

The middle-class mindset focuses on retirement. They believe that sometime in the future, in order to stop being productive, they will stop doing. This concept has a specific date associated with it.

The wealthy focus on the concept of time freedom. They create freedom of time, location, and association through financial and economic freedom. They decide whether they stop working or not and for how long.

The middle-class mindset focuses on tangibles. They look at stuff—things, cars, houses, toys, boats...

The wealthy mindset focuses on intangibles. They focus on innovative thinking, ideas, concepts, and relationships. They have the freedom of thought, to think in any direction they choose, and often the by-product are things.

The Magic Numbers for Real Estate Entrepreneurs

There are a few numbers that I consider magic numbers, when it comes to time management and goal achievement. They are ten, three, and a quarter.

If you focus on how you use these numbers, it can help you in your planning. It is really easy to get lost in the weeds when it comes to developing your real estate business, but if you use this strategy, it will help you.

The first number is ten. When we do planning we want to focus on ten-year goals. These ten-year goals come out through vision boards, graphic organizers. or other tools that help us to envision the future that we want for ourselves.

The next number is three. Once we have developed long-term goals, we break it down into the next three years. By focusing on the near future, it is easier to push ourselves towards much larger goals.

Using the three-year goals, we create quarterly plans. This allows us to focus on those three-year goals in smaller chunks. Having ninety-day goals, rather than yearly goals, helps to ensure that we complete the goals that we set out. Often, when people set annual goals they start them in the beginning of January and don't look at them again until December. But when you focus on ninety-day goals (three months), you are setting goals and refreshing them in that ninety-day period.

Within your quarterly goals, you should set three priorities. These three priorities are geared towards your three-year goals. You will also have different areas that you focus on each quarter. You should also set a challenge for yourself to achieve in that quarter, which takes you out of your comfort zone.

Each week you'll focus on three priorities that move you closer to your quarterly goals. It's much easier to focus on the goals than it is to focus on ten or twenty goals in one week. It's also much easier for you to get those goals completed, if they are not a huge list of to-do items but something that you can focus on each week.

Thinking About Where You Are Right Now

One activity that I highly recommend that everyone does is to complete a Wheel of Life chart. This is a great activity to do before you do any type of long-term planning.

You can see an example of a wheel below. You are going to rate yourself on each section of the wheel from 1 to 10, 1 being the worst and 10 being the best. This is for you to be honest with yourself and does not need to be shared with anyone.

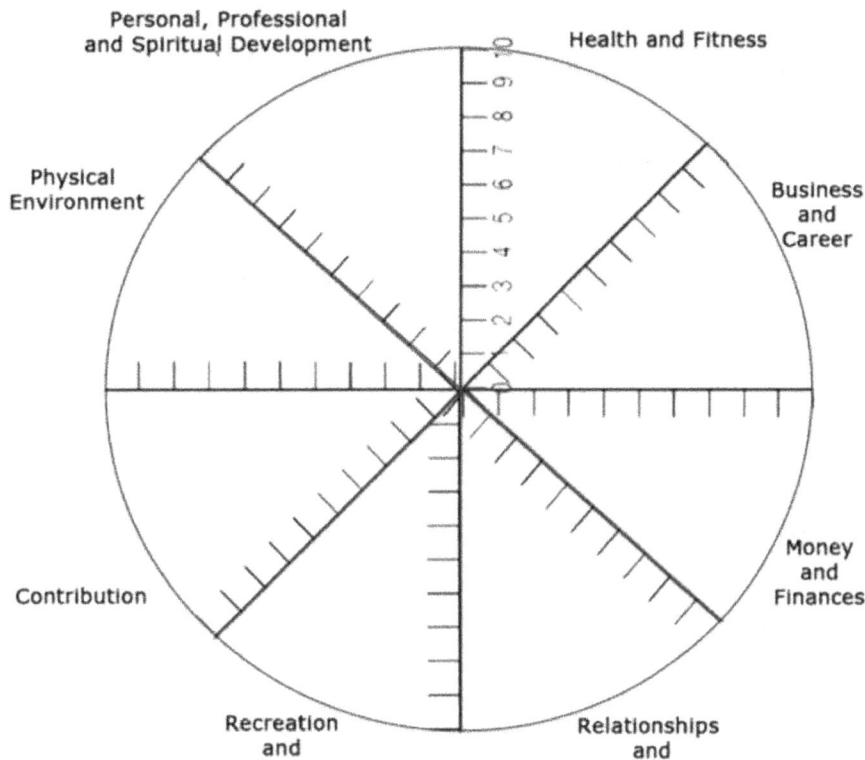

Once you have completed this activity, you will notice some areas of your life with a really low rating and other areas with an extremely high rating. After completing the wheel you may wish to consider bringing up areas that are on the extremely low side to help rebalance yourself. I never suggest bringing down any areas that are high on the wheel.

The Secret Sauce to Your Success - Your Personal BHAGs

"Most people underestimate what they can do in ten or twenty years and overestimate what they can do in one year." ~ Tony Robbins

BHAG stands for Big Hairy Audacious Goal, an idea outlined in the book, *Built to Last: Successful Habits of Visionary Companies* by Jim Collins and Jerry Porras. According to Collins and Porras, a BHAG is a long-term goal that guides your core values and purpose. For you, a long-term goal might be the things you want to achieve ten years from now.

Some people have trouble thinking in terms of decades, it's much easier for them to think in a few months or one-year period. If that sounds like you, one strategy that has worked with past coaching clients is to have them take a weekend trip away from friends and family to spend time thinking about this alone. They must leave their phone, computer, and technology behind and spend time thinking.

Remember, this is a big deal. At the very least, spend a few hours taking a walk by yourself and think about what your future is going to look like.

Questions to ask yourself:

If you were to travel ten years into the future, describe what you see?
What are the things that you are doing every day?
What do you really enjoy?
What does your week look like?
What does your month look like?
What does your year look like?

Some people like to write a letter from their future self-describing what they see. Others like to use graphic organizers or vision boards to help outline exactly what their future looks like. Still, others will write their own obituary of what they would want others to say about them.

It is very important that you do not address **How** you are going to achieve any of these goals. Only think through on what you want to do, where you are, and why you are doing it.

When thinking about this future self don't just focus on one aspect of your life. This is not just about your finances. Think about Business/Professional Life, Finances, Health and Fitness, Relationships, Personal and Professional Development, and Contribution/ Faith.

Once you complete your long-term vision, you have a direction, this is what your other plans are going to be built upon.

Helping You to Achieve Success - Post Your Goals and Vision

Achieving your BHAG takes time and constant motivation. You need to have your goals in a place that you can see it every day, whether it is a vision board in a place that you sit at or the background of your desktop/laptop computer.

Some people like to post their goals by the mirror that they use in the morning. That way they can see their goals each and every day and are reminded of what they are working towards.

However you decide on doing it, posting your goals in a written or visual format where they can easily be seen is a great way to help you to keep focused. Also, if other people see your goals, a conversation ensues, which also helps you to gain clarity by sharing your vision with other people and also helps you through accountability.

Use Affirmations Daily

We will often have an unconscious voice that sits at the back of our mind which tells us something about ourselves. Often, it can relate to our confidence level, as well as how we relate to other people. You can discipline yourself by using affirmations to help you to develop that unconscious voice.

Here is an example of one such affirmation. "I understand success comes from the implementation of knowledge not the acquisition of it. I will capture the ideas that resonate with me and apply them to my life. This is what Action Takers do, and I am an Action Taker."

I have met many successful real estate entrepreneurs that use affirmations to help them to succeed at their goals.

In order to create an affirmation, you can start using the words "I am." Remember that you are talking in the present tense and only use positive messaging to yourself. Make sure that the statement is brief and specific. And make sure that you are only referring to yourself in the affirmation. I like to focus on specific skills that I am working on.

When creating an affirmation, think about your big hairy audacious goal and the underlying skills that are required in order to achieve it. Create an affirmation that helps you to achieve the long-term goals.

The process of using an affirmation is quite simple. Just take a deep breath, stand in front of a mirror, and look yourself in the eye. Repeat the affirmation that you have created for yourself. And do that three or four times. A great time to do this is in the morning when you wake up.

Know Your Freedom Number

Here is a simple formula that changed my life. I didn't really understand what it meant when I started investing in real estate but as I continued to grow as a real estate entrepreneur it made a huge difference in the ability for me to create freedom for myself.

Real Estate Income = Total Personal Expenses + Monthly Savings + Investment Contributions

This Is Your Financial Freedom Number

Step 1: Calculate Your Monthly Personal Expenses

Take some time to make a list and calculate all the things that you spend your money on every month. Here is an example:

	Monthly
Mortgage	$1,800
Property Taxes	400
Insurance Car/Home	200
Groceries	$600
Utilities	$400
Phone	$100
Internet/Cable	$200
Gas	$200
Entertainment	$300
Childcare	$500
Other	$100
	$4,800

In this example, the total amount of monthly expenses is $4800.

Step 2: Add Your Monthly Savings and Investment Contributions

Now when you take the personal expenses number, multiply it by 10 percent, and add that new amount to your total. That will give you a bit of a buffer and also allow you to accommodate for inflation on any additional expenses.

This would be an additional $480 using the previous monthly personal expenses example.

Step 3: Your Financial Freedom Number

Once you add all of these together, you get a number that identifies what you need in order to create financial freedom for yourself.

Using the previous steps, an example would be **$5280 as the financial freedom number.**

The resources that you are currently using to get this financial freedom number is from your head and your hands. It is you that is the asset that others are using in order to create the income that you need. Instead of focusing on yourself as the income source, what if you focused on using real estate, business, or investment assets to create this income.

Your goal is to use these alternate assets to replace yourself as the income source to get to your financial freedom number.

Phases of Real Estate Investing - Where Are You?

Phases of Real Estate Investing

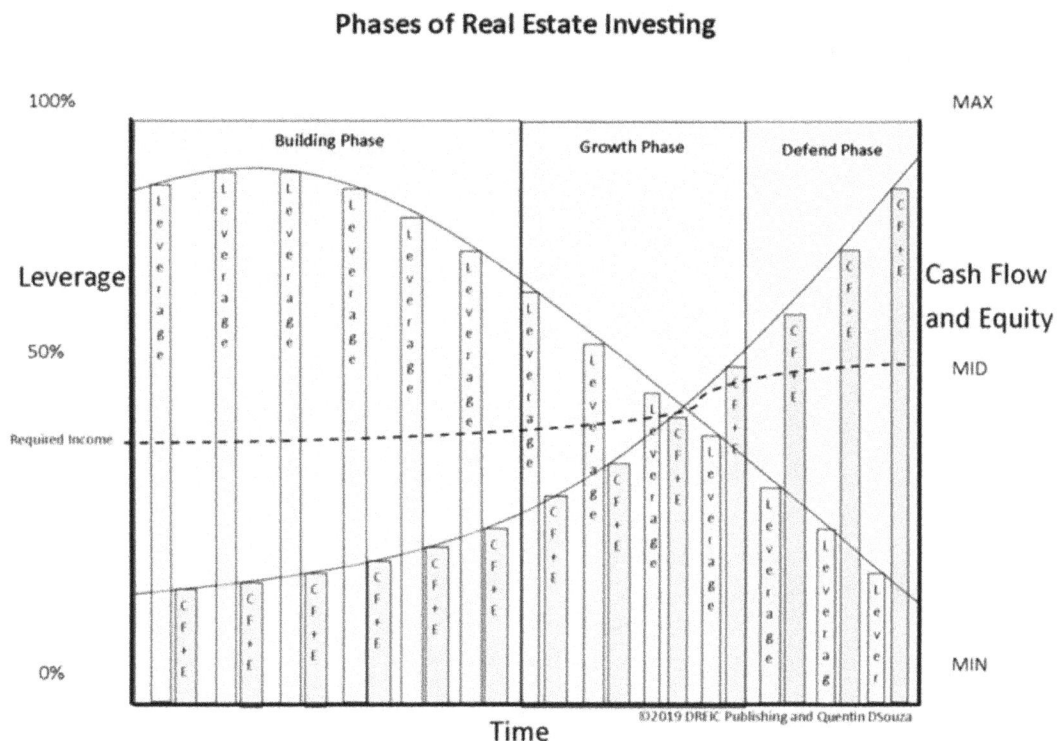

Many investors go through three distinct phases while investing in real estate. Of course, this will depend on your goals. For example, if they are planning on using the funds as their primary income source, how these investors do their purchases and think of investing is quite different and distinct, depending on the phase that they are in. There are many ways that you can skip through phases. If you are just starting out in investing, most likely you start in the building phase, unless you have inherited a number of rental properties, then that might push you into the growth phase.

Required Income

The required income is the income that is necessary for the real estate investor to survive that would include income that is necessary for food, transportation, housing, as well as all the necessities in life. This amount increases over time with inflation and can change depending on the person and how they live. Typically, you see that the real estate income surpasses the required income at some point in the growth phase of the real estate investing journey.

One thing to keep in mind, the phases of investing are really looking from the lens of buy-and-hold perspective. Other types of income like rent-to-owns, flipping, wholesaling, and lending are more active, job like income, or these strategies require you to continue to purchase or find new assets to replace existing ones. Buy-and-hold investments are much more passive income source.

The Building Phase

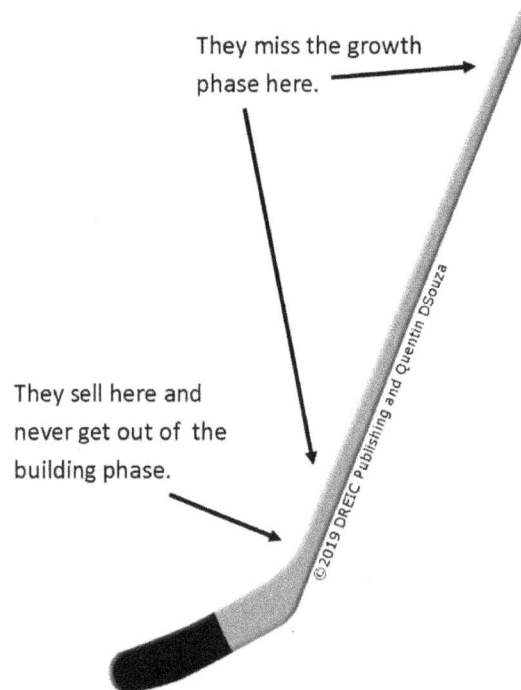

They miss the growth phase here.

They sell here and never get out of the building phase.

©2019 DREIC Publishing and Quentin DSouza

What is distinctive about this stage is that the sheer number of investors who never make it out of this phase. Like one very smart real estate investor and friend told me a long time ago, the investors who never get out of this phase sell at the base of the hockey stick and never realize the much bigger gains that happen in the growth phase on the shaft of the stick.

Leverage is much higher in this phase and the amount of cash flow and equity is lower in the building phase. At this stage many investors will purchase one to three properties and will either start building their team, processes, and procedures in order to build a real estate business or become solo investors and focus on doing all the tasks themselves. If the real estate investor focuses on doing all of the roles themselves, it will take years before they move into the growth phase of their investing. Others who learn to build a business, get education, use mentors, hire a team, and move into adding processes and procedures will move quickly into the next phase.

The Growth Phase

This phase comes with a change in the amount of cash flow and equity that is generated from the real estate business. Often, but not always, leverage starts decreasing and equity and cash flow increase. This can be characterized by equity and cash flow exceeding the amount of mortgages in the portfolio.

In the growth phase, the return on equity is often decreasing. That does not necessarily mean that real estate investors are deleveraging. They may continue to recapitalize on equity through refinances, selling assets, or using secondary financing to build and grow their real estate portfolio.

Often, the growth phase is characterized by more advanced purchase and financing strategies, as well as the ability to use co-venture partnerships(JVs) in order to help with the building in the initial growth phase. Often, in the midst of the growth phase is where we see the required income surpassed by the income from the real estate portfolio, as well as from other streams of income.

The Defend Phase

This stage is where you will find older real estate investors who have been investing for a long time. Their mortgages are often below 50 percent of the value of the property and have lots of equity because of that. These investors receive solid cash flow from their properties. Usually, these real estate investors are enjoying the fruits of their labor or doing one of three things—giving vendor-take-back mortgages to other investors in the building phase or in the process of selling various assets to liquidate or structuring their real estate portfolio in order to pass on their real estate assets and help their children or heirs skip the building phase and move directly into the growth phase of investing.

Where Are You?

Depending on where you are in your real estate investing journey, it will affect the decisions that you make when it comes to strategy, financing, taking on partnerships, growing your portfolio, or investing in different areas.

What I have noticed about the real estate investors that continue to succeed in moving into different phases is that they are always taking action, continually interested in learning more, working on developing themselves, and growing in new and different ways. This is particularly a definitive characteristic of real estate investors who are moving from the building to the growth phase or the growth to the defend phase.

If you are serious about becoming a full-time real estate investor, it's possible to move into the growth phase in five years or less depending on your commitment level and the actions you take.

What Real Estate Strategy to Focus On?

I'm not sure how many times I have heard the term "passive income" and "real estate" together over the last sixteen years at various events and presentations—but it is definitely a lot. It seems that many gurus tout the benefits of investing in real estate by stating that real estate is more like mailbox money that comes to you every month.

Different Real Estate Investment Passive Income

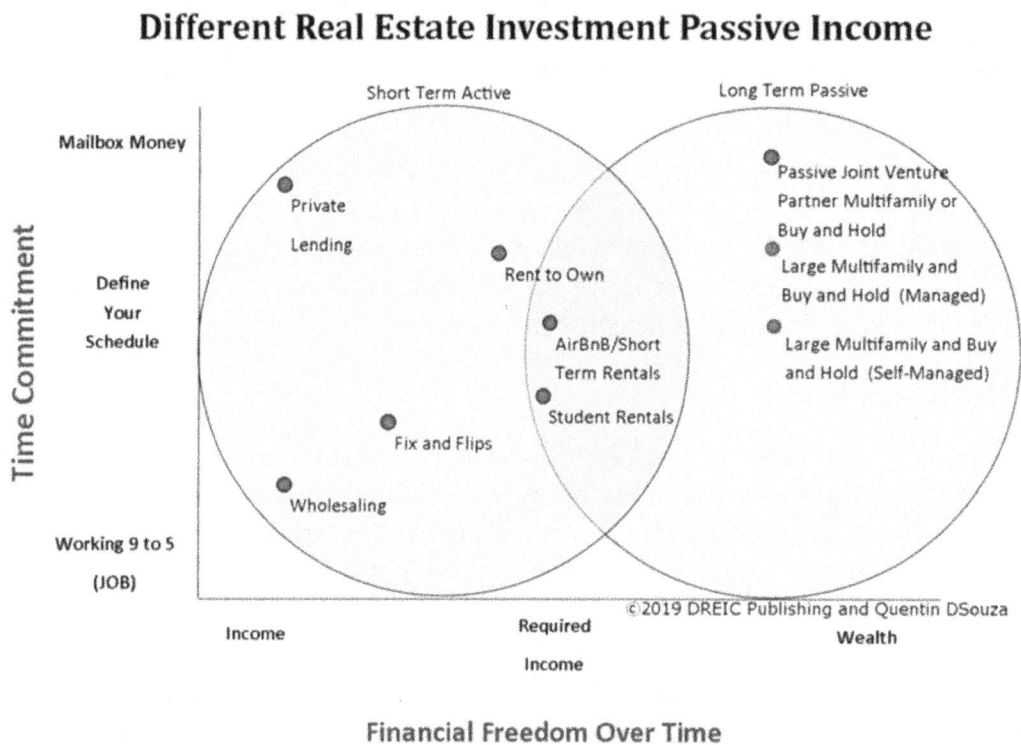

Financial Freedom Over Time

While it's true that real estate is more passive than working a nine-to-five job, there are many pieces that come together that require you to buy it, manage it, or sell it that are not so passive. I don't believe there is anything that is truly passive that doesn't require some time for you to manage it to some extent or another.

There are also some assumptions here—that long term for the buy and hold and multifamily strategies are greater than ten years, are located in solid appreciating areas, with good future investment prospects and cash flow positive assets. And short term is defined as less than five years.

While this is not a definitive guide, it should help to put you into the mindset that you need when it comes to choosing a particular investing strategy in real estate. Also keep in mind there are always tools, team members, and techniques that will help you to minimize your workload and help your real estate empire run smoothly. But that does not eliminate your requirement from managing those things. In fact, if you don't manage those three things then it will affect the success of your real estate business.

On the left-hand side of the graph **"Time Commitment" helps to identify the amount of work necessary to carry out the strategy.** So if it is more job-like it will be lower down on the chart, if it is closer to mailbox money the time commitment is less so it appears higher on the graph.

The bottom of the graph **"Financial Freedom Over Time" helps to identify whether the strategy is focused on income or focused on long-term wealth.** Income is not wealth itself but is part of the process. It is that amount of money that someone receives on a regular or semiregular basis. Wealth for our purposes is related more closely to net worth and is often a byproduct of high income producers but not necessarily.

It is impossible for me to encapsulate every variation of every strategy and put it on the graph. This is only an interpretation.

It is certainly possible to have some strategies that started off as income but turning to long-term wealth. For example, you might have a rent-to-own where the tenant/buyer does not purchase using the option agreement and the property turns into a long-term rental. It is also possible to have strategies like Airbnb, short-term rentals, and student rentals that have long-term passive components. That is why they overlap in the center of the graph.

Short-Term Active

So when we look at the short-term active real estate investment strategies, we are looking at the amount of work to income generated. Let's look at a couple of these strategies in order to understand what I mean by short term.

Wholesaling is a strategy that is often something that you hear in courses that are sold by real estate education companies as a beginner strategy. You basically get an undervalued property with equity under contract with the seller and assign it to another buyer for an assignment fee, which could be $1,000 to $25,000 or more. But the amount of work required to get a wholesaling business going and focusing on the strategy really requires a lot of day-to-day effort, consistent marketing, and networking. Those who do it successfully are often quite busy and usually use other strategies in conjunction with the lead generation that comes from wholesaling. They might do a fix and flip project or add a long-term, buy-and-hold rental to their portfolio.

Let's face it, fix and flip projects are one of the sexiest types of real estate investing. That's why you see it on all the television shows. Making big money now is the perception. Anyone who mentions that they are flipping a property at a real estate investor meeting seems to get instant respect. Basically, what you're doing is taking a house that needs work, increasing the value of the property, and then reselling it quickly, hopefully for a profit.

Often, private lending is one of the most passive of the active income category, depending on the length of time that you are lending funds. One of the challenges with lending is that you are constantly seeking new projects to lend on because the borrower exits the mortgage. The lender then must seek another project and do their due diligence to lend again. There are always ways to make it more passive by using a mortgage agent or broker or mortgage investment corporation, although you have to watch out for the taxes if you aren't structured properly. The higher amount that you are lending, the more you move to the right in the income category of the chart as compared to other active strategies.

Long-Term Passive

Long-term passive strategies are really buy-and-hold projects that are held for a long period of time. The amount of capacity usually depends on whether the properties are self-managed or managed by a professional property management company. Even though there may be a professional property management company working the long-term passive, investors still must manage the company.

The most passive in the long-term wealth category is a passive joint venture partner. That basically is somebody who is providing the financing and/or funding the real estate project but doesn't take an active role in the day-to-day management of the asset. Just like having a property manager, you need to take some time to manage your joint venture partner.

Success Has a Squiggly Path

"Those who never make mistakes work for those of us who do." ~ Henry Ford

Sometimes it feels like every decision you make you are taking two steps forward and one step back. It is important to remember and celebrate the progress that you are making because you are overall moving closer to your goals. Success is never a straight line—there are often ups and downs in investing in real estate.

One of the things that I often say to myself when I get into a challenging time is **"If it were easy everyone would do it."**

I've had days where we had just finished doing a beautiful basement suite conversion, when I didn't realize that there was a high water table in the area and the basement flooded. I could have blamed a whole number of people but in the end every decision that is made is my responsibility. As a real estate entrepreneur you are in business for yourself.

I decided what to buy, I decided who to listen to, and I decided to move forward with the basement conversion. Going forward, I changed my process and checklist to ensure that there were no water issues in any basements. It's something that I learned and something that helped me to ensure I would never commit the same mistake again.

Try to look at your challenges as a learning experience that helps you to create future success.

Developing Your Real Estate Investment Rules

I have found that throughout my real estate investing career that certain rules have come about from different experiences that I have had or that have been shared with me by other real estate investors whom I respect. Those rules help to inform my practice and help continue to allow me to grow in a way to avoid past mistakes as well as to focus on future success. Everyone should be developing rules as they go along as to what to purchase, who to listen to, and how to scale their business.

Here are a few examples of rules.

1. Buildings Depreciate, Land Appreciates

One of the criteria I use to evaluate a particular property is the cost of constructing that same property today. But I also want to remember that land is what becomes more valuable over time more than the building itself. Sticks and bricks depreciate just like any asset if they are not maintained well. The land that surrounds the property is what is really appreciating over time.

2. Buy Land, Not Air

In my area of southern Ontario, there is a real push for investors into condominium developments in high-rise towers. This is great for cities because they are able to intensify the tax base and also house more people on a smaller amount of land. If you think about the previous rule where I believe land appreciates and buildings depreciate, what percentage of the land is actually owned by a condominium owner in a high-rise tower. It is a very small portion of the land.

3. Buy Older, By the New

One of the things that I like to do is look at areas where there is a lot of new development happening and purchasing older properties that are close to those new developments. The new developments often help to increase the value of the older properties. If you find an older property that requires a lot of work, you are able to increase its potential to gain additional value over the long term through the location where it was purchased.

4. Buy Properties with Equity

When purchasing properties, I look for opportunities in order to solve problems of potential sellers. Whether this is repairs that need to be done to the property or helping a seller move quickly or take a much longer time to move in order to solve a particular problem, in order to do this I often will ask for a lower price. By being able to have a lower cost for the repair or solving the problem, I'm able to gain equity on a deal.

5. Focus on What to Invest in, Not When to Invest

Trying to time the market is a day trading stock market mentality. It is very challenging to time the market to exactly where the market is going to go. It's more important to own for a longer period of time in the market rather than time went to purchase a property or once sell property. Instead of doing that, I focus on a particular type of investment that I want to find and add to my portfolio.

What are your real estate investment rules? Why?

Perceived Risk Versus Real Risk

We are in a world with an abundance of information. The amount of videos and audio that are available to download and consume could take you multiple lifetimes and still not get through all the material. It's very interesting to be able to access contrarian views on the same topic. This allows you to examine both sides of an argument and come up with your own decision as to what approach you're going to take. This is true with what you invest in as well as how you decide to invest in the future.

One thing that you need to keep in mind is what is perceived risk and what is a real risk. A perceived risk could be something like the US dollar disappearing and being replaced with digital currency. Although this is in the realm of possibility, it is also unlikely based on the past.

Then there is risk that it is highly unlikely. Let's think about all of the zombie apocalypse movies that are out there. What is the likelihood of this actually occurring in real life? It is quite low.

There is a real comparison to the rental market. For example, there are lots of online media that will lead you down the path of believing that rent can drop 50 percent even in a rent controlled market. What is the real risk of this happening versus the perceived risk?

A real risk would be along the lines of what would have occurred historically in the past. You might think that interest rates increase over the next year by 2 percent or property prices decrease over the next year by 10 percent or expenses increase by 10 percent over the next year because of the jump in property taxes. These would be considered real risks and when you are doing your assessment of a potential project keep in mind real risks because it is near impossible to identify all the perceived risks that are out there and it would prevent you from moving forward on anything.

Moving Your Big Goals into Digestible Quarterly Planning

We spent a lot of time thinking about the big picture. Now we are going to start to take that big picture and break it down into the right amount of tasks in order to get things done. It's time to take these goals and break them down into a quarterly planning process.

CHAPTER 3

Your Quarterly Plan

"Successful people don't wait for the elevator in life; they take the stairs." ~ Unknown

Making Shift Happen

The challenge with goal setting is to find something that works well for you. Over my life, I had set many goals for myself but was unable to achieve those goals until I made a shift in my planning process. I would make goals in January that I had planned to achieve over the year. It is almost as if humans are programmed to forget annual goals after the first three months of setting the goal.

I moved from an annual to a quarterly planning process. By making this shift, I was able to chunk down my goals into more manageable pieces. This helped me to move closer to my long-term vision, but I felt that the progress that was being made was much better than when I was looking at my goals annually.

I encourage all real estate entrepreneurs to use a ninety-day time frame to establish quarterly goals. They can use an accountability partner to help keep them on track, more about that later. Once these quarterly goals are established, you can bring these goals down into your weekly plan.

In 2008, my plan was to have a cash flow of $5,000 a month in order to quit my full-time job. I had set that as a ten-year goal at the time. That meant that in order to achieve that goal I would need to ensure that I generated a new $500 per month in cash flow each year for the next ten years.

At the time I was making that plan, I was able to get 100 percent financing from CMHC for residential purchases for rental properties. If I could pick up one property per quarter, I would be able to gain just over $125 cash flow per month on each new property. If I picked up four properties in a year, I would be able to achieve my goal. So instead of focusing on purchasing forty properties, I simply focused on purchasing one property for that quarter.

I was able to achieve my goal in five years instead of ten years with fewer properties but my long-term plan in conjunction with my quarterly goal helped me to achieve what I had set out to do. It also made me aim higher and think bigger when it came to my ten-year goals. I also realized the power of working on those goals quarterly.

The Art and Science of Tying Your Quarterly Goals into Your Big Why

In the previous section I helped you to see the importance of breaking down your big goals into goals that can be achieved each quarter but what you did not get is the importance of that long-term goal. At that time, my belief was that $5000 per month was my **Freedom Number.** Once I got to that number in cash flow, it opened up the door for me to do many other things.

I could leave my profession as a school teacher, focus on my passions, start working on the collection of business ideas that I had collected over the years, and decide to scale my real estate business even more. The ability to double my income came back to my big why of creating financial independence for me and intergenerational wealth for my family.

Going through the **Big Why** exercise in the previous chapter helps you to identify with the big picture and your long-term goals. Taking those goals and chunking them down into a quarterly goal that is easily measurable makes it easier to identify whether the goal was achieved or not.

For example, making an additional $125 per month on each new property added to the portfolio each quarter. Either I achieved the goal or I didn't achieve the goal. I don't have a goal that can be interpreted differently on a different day. I have not said something like "My goal is to be happier this quarter than last quarter." There is so much subjectivity to that goal, it is hard to know what that means from day to day. Instead, if I set a goal for meditating thirty minutes every day, where the result would be a greater happiness, I can measure whether the meditation was done or not done. Make sure that your goals are specific and measurable.

There is a great mnemonic device that is used related to goal setting—SMART. Each letter reminds you of something different. It is often used in goal setting.

- *Specific* – target a specific area for improvement.
- *Measurable* – quantify or at least suggest an indicator of progress.
- *Achievable* – state what results can realistically be achieved, given available resources.
- *Relevant* – ensure that it focuses on a particular product or client profile.
- *Time-related* – specify when the result(s) can be achieved.

Specific

The criteria stresses the need for a specific goal rather than a more general one. This means the goal is clear and unambiguous. To make goals specific, they must tell a person exactly what's expected, why it's important, who's involved, where it's going to happen, and which is important.

A specific goal will usually answer the five "W" questions:

- What: what do I want to accomplish?
- Why: specific reasons, purpose, or benefits of accomplishing the goal.
- Who: who is involved?
- Where: identify a location.
- Which: identify requirements and problems.

Measurable

Measuring progress toward the attainment of a goal. The thought behind this is that if a goal is not measurable it is not possible to know whether you are making progress toward success. Measuring progress is supposed to help you to stay on track and reach its target dates.

A measurable goal will usually answer questions such as:

- How much?
- How many?
- How will I know when it is accomplished?

Achievable

Your goals are realistic and also achievable. It may stretch your comfort level in order to achieve it. That is, your goals are neither out of reach nor super easy to achieve. When you identify goals that are most important to you, you begin to figure out ways you can make them come true. You develop the attitudes, abilities, skills, and financial capacity to reach them.

An achievable goal will usually answer the question, "How?"

- How can the goal be accomplished?
- How realistic is the goal based on other constraints?

Relevant

Choose goals that matter—make sure that they connect with your Big Why and your Long-Term Goals. Many times you will need support to accomplish a goal: resources, technical assistance, or someone to show you where the roadblocks are and how to avoid them.

Relevant goals are in alignment with other goals and to be considered relevant.

A relevant goal can answer yes to these questions:

- Does this seem worthwhile?
- Is this the right time?
- Are you the right person?

Time-Bound

Grounding your goals within a quarterly plan automatically creates a time frame, giving you a target date. A commitment to a deadline helps you focus your efforts on completion of the goal on or before the due date. This part of the SMART goal criteria is intended to prevent goals from being overtaken by the day-to-day tasks that you need to do and to establish a sense of urgency.

A time-bound goal will usually answer the question:

- When?
- What can I do six months from now?
- What can I do six weeks from now?
- What can I do today?

Doing Out of Your Comfort Zone

Although the title sounds a little off, it is what I mean. When people say you need to get out of your comfort zone in order to grow—you actually need to do things out of your comfort zone. Usually, it requires some sort of action on your part in order to take you out of your comfort zone.

Let me give you an example. I had never talked to any potential joint venture partners before and I was very interested in growing my portfolio and the only way that I could think of at the time was to send an email letting people know what I was doing. I didn't know how many people would be reading the message so I worded it as if I was talking to 1,000 people. When I sent out the email, I would use the blind carbon copy [BCC] in order to send the email to all the recipients that I knew. I think at the time it was about twenty people. I felt very uncomfortable talking about myself and the different things that I was doing but I knew if I was to find a partner I had to do something different. I had sent the email once a month, sometimes twice a month, for six months without any indication whether the emails were being read or not. Finally, in the seventh month I was contacted by a potential joint venture partner and it helped to start me on my journey working with co-ventures in projects. But if I did not take that first step of sending emails to people telling them about myself and what I was doing, I would never have gotten to the point where I am today.

You need to always remember that what got you to where you are now is not going to be the same as what is going to get you to the next stage. You are going to need to do different things than you have done before, whatever that may be. When you are doing something out of your comfort zone, usually there is some physical feeling at the bottom of your stomach that tells you that you're doing something uncomfortable. The only way to get comfortable doing it is doing it again and again and again. Never ever ever ever give up!

Quarterly Challenge

What challenge will take you out of your comfort zone this quarter?

- [ ] Get a 20 + Unit Building under Contract and Leverage Partnerships and Network to raise the funds for this project

Face Your Fears

Over-Commit
Compelling Reason
Focus On Next Step
Join Group
Act – Don't Think
Ask For Help

There are a few strategies that you can use in order to face your fears. Whether that is public speaking or putting in your first offer on a rental property.

Overcommit - The first strategy is to overcommit. So let's say that your goal is to create an additional $500 a month in cash flow from your real estate portfolio for the quarter. Instead of using the number $500 in your quarterly plans, set the goal to $1,000 per month in additional cash flow.

Give Yourself a Compelling Reason - It is much easier to face your fears when there is a compelling underlying reason for you to do something. For example, if you know that your job is going to be terminated in two years you will be more motivated to create another stream of income for yourself. The compelling reason, like for me, could be something as simple as wanting to create a better life for your immediate family than what you had growing up.

Focus on the Next Step – Often, I find that real estate investors get too caught up with the number of doors or number of properties that they have set as a goal for themselves in order to achieve what they want to do. Instead of focusing on a big number of properties or number of doors, just focus on the next property—that's it. When you are focusing on the next step, you are more likely to achieve it than if you're trying to focus on a much bigger picture all the time.

Join a Group - There are lots of groups available that can help you to learn about real estate investing and will include a number of peers who would be able to help you to achieve your goals. If you attend meetings or clubs or associations that have people who have already achieved the goals that you are looking to achieve, you are more likely to achieve those goals yourself. You are more easily able to face any fears that you have with that particular group of people.

Act Don't Think - Sometimes this can be the hardest thing to do. Your mind will often tell you not to do something but if you can force your body to do it you are more likely to face your fear. Let me give you an example of this. This often happens in a variety of sports where your mind tells you that this doesn't make sense for you to do it but you tell your body to do it anyways. One example might be skydiving, forcing yourself to leave a perfectly good plane with a parachute on your back by forcing your body to do it anyways.

Ask for Help - With all the information that's available everywhere, it is easy for people to access information more than ever before. The challenge is always finding people who are the true experts when it comes to whatever it is that you are learning. I always suggest that you visit meetings in clubs and ask the most experienced investors what they are doing and how they are doing it. Whenever you go to meetings or networking events, come with questions and ask for help. This could also mean simply taking another investor out to lunch or dinner, or paying for their time.

How Does a Seasoned Real Estate Investor Approach Risk?

Risk is one of the most misunderstood terms when discussing investing in any asset class. If you can understand what risk means, you will see as I have seen, that seasoned real estate investors are one of the least risky investors.

If you were to ask someone who is not a seasoned investor, what they needed to do in order to see bigger profits in their investments, they might say that taking bigger risks is what leads to more profits.

Compared to a seasoned real estate investor's perception of what is riskier—investing in rental property or keeping money in the bank, you might be surprised by their response of buying rental property.

Usually, when people think about risk when it comes to their investments, they are really thinking about whether or not there is a chance to lose their money. This is really a misappropriation of the term "risk." It probably has come from some financial planner providing a risk tolerance questionnaire that asked them whether they considered themselves risk-averse, average, or above average. And it relates directly to the legal liability incurred by the financial planner losing their money.

But that isn't what risk is when you are coming from an investment perspective.

Let's look at an example outside of real estate—skydiving.

You might consider this sport as one of the most risky activities out there. From your perspective, they are jumping out of a perfectly good plane from thousands of feet up in the air with just a parachute. Risky you say.

From the perspective of the skydiver, they might not see their sport as risky at all. They have the proper equipment, go through a number of pre-jump steps, and do their safety procedures throughout the process. This helps to prepare them and ensure that the skydive is going to be safe. They know what they need to do in order to jump safely and they do it. When you compare driving a car to skydiving, you are actually thousands of times more likely to die in a car crash than skydiving.

So **risk is contextual** and is based on the **knowledge and experience** of the person who is doing the activity.

The ability to know what to measure is the **key here.** A seasoned real estate investor understands that risk is the ability to **measure uncertainty** and **measure the probability of profits.**

He or she may use spreadsheets and calculators to help them get a better understanding of the uncertainties of a specific investment and **apply criteria to it** (i.e. cash flow, ROI, cash on cash, or other criteria).

Seasoned real estate investors speak to other investors, listen to economists, read books and articles, and keep track of different trends to be able to **understand what different possibilities may affect them**.

They make decisions based on their understanding of these measurements.

Because they focus on the probability of profits, they are more confident about the results that the investments will provide. The seasoned real estate investor understands and can measure uncertainty.

But how does a seasoned real estate investor approach risk? Really there are three approaches, not just one.

1. Avoid the Risk

This is quite simply not making the investment at all. It's much easier to avoid a bad situation. Not every deal is a great deal. There are many variables that go into making a successful deal. And sometimes one of those variables is skewed unfavorably against the investor. Knowing when to say no is just as important as saying yes.

2. Reduce the Risk

Reducing the risk means that the seasoned real estate investor will use their knowledge and skills to create a margin of safety within the investment. This will add intrinsic value and look for solutions to ensure that the investment has a probability of profit.

You hear this in common metaphors like, you make money when you buy the property.

It is having that knowledge and understanding of what to do with the property, which helps to create an additional margin of safety from the buy.

For example, if you were to take an illegal accessory apartment in a detached house and through a few little fixes create a legal accessory apartment. You would have reduced the risk of a neighbor complaining to the city and shutting down the accessory apartment and be able to create value that exceeded the cost of the renovations. You would then be able to extract some of this new equity through refinancing the property and lowering the amount of funds that are left in the property. This would increase your return on investment, if by lowering your initial investment. In this one example, you can see that risk is reduced from neighbors, safety, liability, and money.

3. Focus on the Risk

The last approach to risk is very different from reducing the risk of a particular invest-ment. Once you have reduced the risk for an investment you have simply added it to your portfolio and it simply follows the process and procedures that were setup for it.

When you focus on risks you are actively managing it. For a seasoned real estate in-vestor, the property is getting all of your attention.

This could mean that a seasoned investor would sell an asset, having realized that the property was a mistake and needs to be sold off, or that investment has done what it was intended to do and it is time to reap the profits.

A seasoned investor distances themselves from the real estate market and all the emotions that come with it. They measure current uncertainties and the probability of profits as it relates to the property. And then evaluate what needs to be done with the investment.

Centers of Influence

One of the components of the quarterly plan that was inspired by a mentor of mine, Dan Sul-livan. He really focuses your attention away from doing things yourself—instead he asks who will be able to do those tasks for you. **Ask Who, Not How.** These people will be able to help you to achieve your quarterly goals as well as the good peers or team members.

As a real estate entrepreneur, you are constantly going to be pulled in different directions, so it is important to be able to continue with the projects that you have and build a business so that you can scale and grow. Instead of figuring out how you are going to do a particular task, start asking the question of who is going to implement this project or task for me.

When you are focusing on who and not how, you are developing centers of influence who will be able to help you to achieve your quarterly goals

---

Centers of Influence

Who will help you with your three areas of focus this quarter?

M. Jacobs (Realtor)   J. Smith (PM)

__ I. Farber (Realtor)   __ S. Reynolds (PM)

__ E. Abrams (BMO)   __ J. Smith (MF Investor)

Sample Quarterly Plan

Date: _Dec 30/2020_   **Quarterly Plan for Real Estate Action Takers**

Three Areas of Focus This Quarter

Focus #1: _Reposition Exiting Building and Close on 20 Units - Portfolio Growth_

Result: _Increase Cash flow of $1500_

Actions Needed to Get the Result:

☐ Turn over 3 units within Existing Portfolio (+$600)

☐ Make Offers on 5-10 Buildings (Develop relationships with key players) (+$1000 per)

☐ JV Partner Multifamily Overview Sheet and Proforma to 10 People

Focus #2: _Increase Cash Position_

Result: _Free Up Funds for Taxes, New Purchase or to Act As If It Were Cash_

Actions Needed to Get the Result:

☐ USA Portfolio Refinance - Complete Process and Access Funds

☐ Sale of 3 Garden Street Properties - Contact Tenants and Start the Process

☐ Apply for Unsecured LOC and Increase Portfolio Blanket Loan

Focus #3: _Maintain Healthy Lifestyle_

Result: _Weight will be 220 pounds_

Actions Needed to Get the Result:

☐ Running and walking 6x per week

☐ No food or Snacks after 9 pm

☐ Track Daily Food Intake on App

Consistent growth in these three areas helps your real estate portfolio grow.		
Finding	**Funding**	**Financing**
☐ Get 10-20+ Unit building under contract	☐ 2 New JV Partners with 500k+ to invest	☐ Complete Refi of USA Portfolio with Morgan
☐ 10 New Lead sources in apartment building	☐ Have 1 million in Accessible Cash/Credit	☐ Prepare Financing Binder for Apps

Quarter Starts: _Jan 1/2021_   **Quarter Ends:** _March 31/2021_

Quarterly Challenge

What challenge will take you out of your comfort zone this quarter?

☐ Get a 20+ Unit Building Under Contract and Leverage Partnerships and Network to raise the funds for this project

Delegate

What task(s) will you delegate this quarter?

☐ Assistant to do Utilities Processing

☐ Assistant to do monthly Insurance Checklist

Systems and Processes

What task(s) will you systematize this quarter?

☐ End of Month Payment/Late Process Refine

☐ JV Follow-Up Process When Interest is shown in investing

Personal Development

What will you learn this quarter?

☐ Crushing It in Apartment Buildings Book

☐ Secret Life of Real Estate and Banking Book

☐ Definitive Guide to Underwriting Multifamily Acquisitions Book

Centers of Influence

Who will help you with your three areas of focus this quarter?

☐ M. Jacobs (Realtor)   ☐ J. Smith (PM)

☐ I. Farber (Realtor)   ☐ S. Reynolds (PM)

☐ E. Abrams (BMO)   ☐ J. Smith (MF Investor)

Financial/Real Estate Strategy Focus

What financial and/or real estate investment strategy will you focus on this quarter?

☐ Tenant Turnover Push - Use new agreement to end tenancy early with negotiation

☐ JV Partners on Larger Multi-Family Buildings

The 4 REI Freedoms: ✓ Time Freedom   ☐ Location Freedom
✓ Financial Freedom   ✓ Thought Freedom

CHAPTER 4

Your Weekly Plan

"The big hit never comes without a great number of little hits first." ~ John Maxwell

The Week Ahead

Have you ever wondered why some people complain that there are not enough hours in the day and others can complete a PhD while training for a marathon and spending time with their children? We all have the same 189 hours in a week—it is what you do with those hours that are most important. As you achieve more goals, you will start to see that you develop more and become a better you. It is as important as achieving your goals—it can be an inspiration to yourself, family, and your community.

Your quarterly goals is the map that helps you to get to the place where you want to go. The weekly plan is the turn by turn instructions that help you to make the journey. As you achieve more goals, you'll see that you will be able to do more. You will develop more self-confidence and honestly you can become a better you. Not only that but you can be an inspiration to your family and to your community.

When you are doing your weekly plan, I suggest you just pick a time that you can do it each week, either on Sunday evening before you go to bed or Monday morning as soon as you get up. You need to dedicate at least fifteen to twenty minutes in order to plan out a successful week. Once you get into the rhythm of completing a weekly plan, you will see how powerful this will be in helping you to accomplish your quarterly goals. You will see how each week, through the use of your planner, you will be able to make progress on all the goals that you have for the quarter.

A Not To-Do List

One of the powerful things you can do is ensure that you have a not to-do list of items. Most of the time, people think about having to-do lists but it is even more powerful when you reverse it and create not to-do lists.

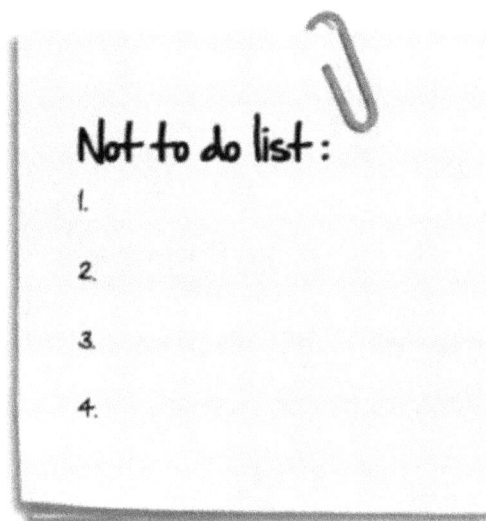

Let's say you are constantly answering your phone and you want to create more time in order to accomplish other things. You should set a rule like, I never pick up the phone when a caller comes in as a private caller. You have realized that 80 percent of the time they're trying to sell you a haircut, duct cleaning, or carpet cleaning, so you decide never to pick up those calls again in the future. That would be adding something to your not to-do list.

Here is an example of a Not To-Do List from Tim Ferriss, author of *The 4-Hour Work-week*.

1. **Do not answer calls from unrecognized phone numbers.**
2. **Do not e-mail first thing in the morning or last thing at night.**
3. **Do not agree to meetings or calls with no clear agenda or end time.**
4. **Do not let people ramble.**
5. **Do not check e-mail constantly—"batch" and check at set times only.**
6. **Do not overcommunicate with low-profit, high-maintenance customers.**
7. **Do not work more to fix overwhelm—prioritize.**
8. **Do not carry a cellphone or CrackBerry 24/7.**
9. **Do not expect work to fill a void that nonwork relationships and activities should.**

As you're not to-do list grows, you will find that time frees up for you and allows you to focus on items that will take you closer to your quarterly goals.

Weekly - Finding, Financing, and Funding (3 Fs)

As a real estate investor, it is important for you to be able to focus on three particular areas each week, if not daily. These three items will continue to increase the scale and scope of your business.

Finding - Deal flow is a challenge for all investors at one time or another. It's great to have opportunities that you can pick up on the MLS or through a realtor, but if you can create other methods of lead generation you will be able to find deals that other people will not be able to produce anywhere. You should make at least one new connection that will help generate opportunities for you each week. Some examples of the tasks that you would do here—networking with landlords, talking to a realtor, meeting with a homeowner who is selling, talking to other investors or contractors, letting them know you are buying properties and what you are looking for.

Funding - We all wish that we had unlimited amounts of money in our own bank account but this is not the case, unless you are a central bank and can print your own money. You can, however, ensure that you are sufficiently funded if you focus on this each week. Funds for your renovations, down payments, joint venture partnerships, or access to cash for private mortgages can help you get that amazing project that you don't want to pass up. For some people this could mean contacting their banks and accessing a line of credit, for other people this could mean being in contact with potential joint venture partners, for still other people this could mean contacting friends or relatives in order to provide private lending on upcoming projects.

This could also mean contacting different financial or mortgage professionals to see If there is a unique product you can access that would give you the ability to get more funds. For example, as your portfolio grows you may be able to take out a portfolio line of credit against several properties in order to access the equity through a secured line of credit with a blanket mortgage. This is a more complex process because it would mean accessing a line of credit across multiple properties but could free up hundreds of thousands of dollars, depending on your portfolio size.

Financing - Real estate investors usually start out working with a particular lender because they have gained the comfort with that financial institution. I can tell you that no matter which financial professional you start with, you will not end up using them forever if you want to continue to grow your portfolio of properties. You'll notice that over time financing arrangements change in every financial institution as well as insurance products that back those institutions. This means that you will be in constant search for lenders that will be able to help you achieve your real estate goals. Focusing on financing each week will help you to do that.

It is important to continue to build relationships with a number of different mortgage professionals, whether they be mortgage brokers, mobile mortgage specialists, or mortgage agents. You will need to contact other real estate investors to see which financial institutions they are working with and see if you can generate some contacts at that institution in order to start building those relationships. This could mean contacting credit unions or other institutions that you may not have any contact with in the past.

Some mortgage brokers have great relationships with a particular financial institution that could give you more flexibility in getting mortgages. I do find that programs for lenders in the real estate investing space change from time to time so being able to have multiple financing options is very useful for real estate investors.

As your portfolio grows, you will find it difficult to finance properties on your own. I once spent six months going to twelve different lenders outside of what was available through the mortgage broker channel in order to find a lender who would refinance a commercial building for me. You would think that it is easier to get financing, as you have properties that unfortunately banks don't look at it that way, they see it as more of a risk. So it becomes more challenging as you have properties in your name. I would spend some time each day getting a no, sometimes a couple weeks, until I finally found a local credit union that would get the refinance completed for me.

Another option that people will use is working to find a mortgage qualifier, who would take a piece of the equity of the deal but would do the mortgage qualification component for you. Meaning that they have the ability to qualify for the mortgage but don't have a down payment or experience with rental properties. Usually, the mortgage qualifier will get an equity component or part of the cash flow of the property in order to qualify for a residential purchase. In the commercial space, it is less likely that a mortgage qualifier would be needed if the net operating income is sufficient for the subject building.

TIP: In the template for the weekly plan you can set a priority for the day and you can pick finding, funding, or financing as your priority in order to keep focused.

Finding	Funding	Financing
Actions this week to find new properties:	Actions this week to access credit, investors or cash:	Actions this week to access private lenders or financing:
☐ Meet seller of 12 Unit Property in Oshawa - Negotiate Offer	☐ Talk to Fan and Peter About JVs	☐ Firm up financing on Burnham

Weekly - Do, Delegating, or Dump It (3 Ds)

In order to move away from being self-employed into creating a business, you must remove items from your plate that you would normally do on a daily or weekly basis. The weekly plan specifies an area where you need to be getting rid of an activity off your plate. This could mean that you are willing to get the action accomplished this week or you're going to give it to somebody else to complete for you or you're not going to do it anymore or at all.

Whatever you choose to do, use the weekly plan in order to help you focus on getting the item or action off of your plate so that you can focus on your higher priority tasks.

For example, if you are somebody who is hands-on on their rental properties and feel like they need to paint their rental properties because it will save them some money, I would assign this to the weekly plan in order to delegate this to a painter. It makes no sense for you to be doing a $20 an hour task. Instead, if you focus on finding a joint venture partner or finding your next property, you are going to be earning thousands of dollars per hour rather than wasting your time on doing a low-level task. Regardless of whether it needs to be done or not, I'm not saying that you should not do emergency items if you are stuck but you should not plan for yourself to do those items. In this case, you should delegate it.

Here are some other examples:

Do - Items that need to be done by yourself today. (Conference call with potential partner.)

Delegate - Items that you need to delegate today. (Letter from engineer about property being sent to building department).
Dump - Stop eating after 9:00 p.m., stop watching reality TV and read a real estate book, stop sleeping in and go for a run—what is getting in the way of productivity.

Do, Delegate, Dump

Actions this week working on your business:

- ☐ Assign End of Month Checklist for Rents to Assistant

Eat That Frog

Each week you should have an item that needs to get completed for that week in order for you to have a successful week. This could be an item that you have been procrastinating on for a while and you are setting a time to ensure that you get it done.

Some examples could be reviewing joint venture agreements, preparing a pro forma of particular properties in order to ensure they follow your investment criteria, or this could be talking with a particular realtor that you have been avoiding. Whatever it is, your plan is to get it done this week. My suggestion is that you focus on getting it done on Monday morning.

Brian Tracy has an interesting concept where he talks about doing the hardest task at the very beginning of the day because it makes it so much easier for you to get that item done. You have the highest amount of willpower at the beginning of the day.

Think of willpower as a battery, as you get later in the day, it becomes harder for that willpower battery to be fully charged and harder to get those items done. That's why you might find that, if you're dieting, that in the evening it becomes harder for you to stick to your diet because you're willpower battery has started to wear down for use all day.

Eat That Frog

What have you been procrastinating on?

- ☐ Submit Plans for Fire Retrofit of Dufferin

Centers of Influence

Each week you need to set aside time to connect with one person who will help you with your three areas of focus for the quarter. These people should already be successful in the goals that you are trying to achieve or have special connections or influence that will help you to achieve your goals. Putting a specific person's name down is important; you should not be putting a general classification of a person's job or profession. You need to put the specific name of a person and make an effort to connect with that person.

Centers of Influence

Actions to develop these relationships:

☐ Lunch with Brian from Mortgage Company

Celebrate Life

What Success Can You Celebrate and What Are You Doing This Week to Do That?

We should always take some time and celebrate the successes that we have had. This does not mean that you need to schedule a party every time you purchase a new house or apartment building. But you should do something different that allows you to celebrate that particular success. It could be going out for dinner or buying a special bottle of wine, whatever it is, those successes should be celebrated.

Another thing that we need to remember to do is that there are many parts to our life that we need to continue to celebrate on a weekly basis. That could be celebrating by having a little bit of extra money to do something with your family or going to a ballgame or spending a little bit of extra time with friends and family. You should always take some time every week to celebrate life with your family and friends, after all, without them your life wouldn't be very exciting.

Celebrate Life

Fun actions this week that focus on the present.

☐ Flying Lesson Number 12 - Stalls

Three Priorities This Week

Each week you should have three priorities that you focus on. Getting these priorities done will make your week an awesome week. These three priorities should tie into your quarterly plan and focus directly on your real estate business.

When you are writing down your priorities make sure that there is something specific about what it is that you need to get completed. For example, you may be purchasing the new apartment building. One of the priorities that will be included would be creating a new corporation and getting financing locked up for the purchase.

You would write:

Use MP Law to Create New Corporation and Get Financing Terms with Meridian Bank.

You should easily be able to tell whether a priority has been completed or not. The more specific you are with a priority, the easier it will be for you to tell whether it has been completed.

Three Priorities This Week

Getting these done will make an awesome week.

☐ Ready for Wednesday presentation for Joint Venture partners - review proforma and credibility binder, think through potential question and answer

☐ Get 3 insurance quotes for Burnham project and compare based on rental property insurance guidelines

☐ Complete financing package with updated binder, with property portfolio, and send to mortgage broker

---

Quarterly Plan

When you are completing your weekly plan, you should take a minute to review your quarterly plans. On your weekly plan, you should include actions that you move your quarterly plan forward. This is not the same as the three priorities that you are going to be completing, rather it would be other items in your quarterly plan. For example, if you are looking to do a new purchase through a private sale, you will need as your focus for the quarter, time investigating different marketing options for private sale lead generation. That will help bring you closer to your goal of getting a private sale.

The actions in this area move you closer towards achieving your focus for the quarter. This could be related to personal development, reading a section from a book, listening to a specific podcast, attending a mastermind to learn something specific in the area of focus for the quarter, or just a phone call with a center of influence who understands the area that you are working on. Whatever it is, the actions that you complete this week will help you to achieve your quarterly goals.

Quarterly Plan

These actions move your quarterly plan forward.

☐ Inform tenants planning to sell Garden street

☐ Complete - Crushing It in Apartment Buildings - on Audible

☐ 5xwalk@8-10km + 2 Runs @ 5 kms + 3 Workouts for 45 min

End of the Week

At the end of the week you should be reviewing what has been completed and what has not been completed. Make sure to check off items that have been completed as you complete them during the week. Circle the items that have not been completed. You need to review why these items have not been completed in order to make sure that they get completed the following week.

Did you not set aside enough time to complete the action? Were you simply trying to avoid the activity? Did you not specify a specific time during the week to complete this item for yourself, so that it has been done? The idea behind this weekly plan is that it helps you to plan out all of your actions for the week and ensures that you have enough time to complete those actions. If you don't spend the time planning out your week, it will be harder for you to get items completed.

Quarterly Plan

These actions move your quarterly plan forward.

☑ Inform tenants planning to sell Garden street

☑ Complete - Crushing It in Apartment Buildings - on Audible

☐ 5xwalk@8-10km + ✓(2 Runs @ 5 kms)+ 3 Workouts ✓ for 45 min ~~Need to schedule~~ time to get to the gym and back

Using an Accountability Partner

Accountability partners support each other in order to keep the weekly items that need to be accomplished at the forefront of each other's minds. They meet each week usually by phone in order to review the past week and share what they are working on for the next week. Weekly meetings are approximately fifteen minutes.

You don't need a partner who lives anywhere near you or is even in the same industry as you. They just need to be available and be consistent. The power comes from you telling other people what your plans are and what you have or have not accomplished.

Here is an example of what the call might look like.

Past—Step 1

1. What you should be sharing is the successes and areas that you made progress over the past week.

2. What were your top three priorities and how successful were you at completing those priorities?

3. How are you doing with your quarterly plan and how are your plans meshing with your long-term goals?

Future—Step 2

1. What are the top three priorities that you are working on this week?

2. How are these priorities tied into your quarterly plans?

3. How are these priorities tied into your long-term goals?

A Few Tips:

Make sure that you keep your agreements with your accountability partner. If you say that you are going to meet at a specific time, then meet.

- Make sure that you complete your weekly update before you contact your accountability partner.
- Be honest with your accountability partner. Remember, they are not your coach. Don't allow yourself to be affected by your partner's failures or lack of action—support them into action.
- Take responsibility for making your accountability partnership work.

Make sure that you have an accountability partner and you have scheduled your accountability call. Check off on your weekly plan that it has been completed or not completed.

Accountability Call ✓Next Call Scheduled ✓Completed

3	**Monday**

Priority: JV Proforma/Binder

6 ---------------
7 Morning Excercise ----
8 ---------------
9 Daily Huddle with EA
10 Accountability partner
11 ---------------
12 Lunch with Brian ---
1 Afternoon Walk
2 Proforma/Binder Prep
3 ---------------
4 ---------------
5 ---------------
6 ---------------
7 Son's Hockey Game
8 ---------------
9 ---------------
10 ---------------

Using the Hourly Grid to Plan Out Your Week

Using the box beside the day of the week, put the number of the day of the month. You can do that for the whole week so that you are on top of each day and you can prioritize what is happening all week.

Below each day of the week include one priority for the day. If you choose to have a date that does not have anything, make sure that you include it as your priority. It is okay to have a day to rest and recharge so that you can be fully present with your family and friends.

Each day is organized from 6:00 a.m. to 10:00 p.m. You can use each line to block off time to complete specific tasks. By attributing specific times to complete specific tasks, you should be able to get those tasks done. All the priorities and items that you have included in your weekly plan should appear somewhere in your hourly grid in order to ensure that it gets completed. Blocking off specific time for you, your task ensures that you are committed to making sure that it's done. I have been using this time blocking for years and have been able to publish three books, not including this one, which have all used time blocking to ensure that time was given to the book in order to make sure that it was completed.

Getting It Done Every Day

In the past, I used Stephen Covey's quadrant for my daily tasks. I found that it was a little overkill but you may find it quite useful. It was a great starting point for what I do now on a daily basis. Stephen Covey would use a piece of paper that he would fold in two quarters, in one corner he would put important and urgent, in another quarter important but not urgent, another quarter not important but urgent, and finally not important but not urgent. These are the tasks that you need to get completed during the day.

Stephen Covey's 4 Quadrants

	Urgent		Not Urgent	
Important	**Quad I**		**Quad II**	
	Activities	**Results**	**Activities**	**Results**
	• Crisis • Pressing Problems • Deadline Driven	• Stress • Burn-out • Crisis management • Always putting out fires	• Prevention, capability improvement • Relationship building • Recognizing new opportunities • Planning, recreation	• Vision, perspective • Balance • Discipline • Control • Few crisis
Not Important	**Quad III**		**Quad IV**	
	Activities	**Results**	**Activities**	**Results**
	• Interruptions, some callers • Some email, some reports • Some meetings • Proximate, pressing matters • Popular activities	• Short term focus • Crisis management • Reputation – chameleon character • See goals/ plans as worthless • Feel victimized, out of control • Shallow or broken relationships	• Trivia, busy work • Some email • Personal social media • Some phone calls • Time wasters • Pleasant activities	• Total irresponsibility • Fired from jobs • Dependent on others or institutions for basics

An example of important and urgent would be a 5:00 p.m. meeting with a business mentor.

An example that is important but not urgent would be anything related to your big hairy audacious goal for the quarter. That is important but not urgent, although getting this done will surely bring you closer to your quarterly goals.

An example of not important but urgent is getting snow tires put on your vehicle, as the winter is approaching.

Not important but not urgent would be finding a gift for your cousin's birthday next month.

One of the things that I have been able to do, and you will be able to do over time, is leverage assistance to help you to get things completed. Usually, items that are in the not important but urgent and not important but not urgent, I will assign to an assistant or virtual assistant to complete for me because of their status but also that it doesn't require me to actually complete the tasks efficiently. So now I really have a list of two important and urgent and important but not urgent for the following day and that's what I would include on a cue card that I use to ensure that things are getting completed.

Now Get Started

It's time for you to get started on completing your first weekly plan. Use everything that was mentioned in the last chapter to help you to get completed.

CHAPTER 5

Quarterly Plan Template

BALANCE SHEET

ASSETS		LIABILITIES	
Total Deposits:		Unsecured LOC:	
Unregistered Investments:		Car and Personal Loans:	
Registered Investments:		Secured Lines of Credit:	
Real Estate Portfolio:		Mortgages:	
Personal Assets:		Other:	
Other:			
Total Assets		Total Liabilities:	
Total Assets -Total Liabilities = **Net Worth:**			

☐ **High Net Worth Canadians**($1M-$5M) ☐ **Mid-Tier Millionaires**($5M-$30M) ☐ **Ultra High Net Worth**($30M+)

INCOME DIVERSITY

1. Salary/Hourly/Commission $_____

2. Real Estate Cash Flow After Expenses $_____

3. Business Profits $_____

4. Intellectual Property Residuals $_____

5. Interest Income $_____

6. Pensions, Benefits, Insurance $_____

7. Dividend Earnings/Options $_____

8. Sale of Assets $_____

9. Private Equity Yield $_____

10. Refinances $_____

11. Other Income $_____

TOTAL $_____

Date: _____   **Quarterly Plan for Real Estate Action Takers**

Three Areas of Focus This Quarter

Focus #1: _____

Result: _____

Actions Needed to Get the Result:

☐

☐

☐

Focus #2: _____

Result: _____

Actions Needed to Get the Result:

☐

☐

☐

Focus #3: _____

Result: _____

Actions Needed to Get the Result:

☐

☐

☐

Consistent growth in these three areas helps your real estate portfolio grow:		
Finding	**Funding**	**Financing**
☐	☐	☐
☐	☐	☐

Quarter Starts: _____ **Quarter Ends:** _____

Quarterly Challenge

What challenge will take you out of your comfort zone this quarter?

☐

Delegate

What task(s) will you delegate this quarter?

☐

☐

Systems and Processes

What task(s) will you systematize this quarter?

☐

☐

Personal Development

What will you learn this quarter?

☐

☐

☐

Centers of Influence

Who will help you with your three areas of focus this quarter?

☐   ☐

☐   ☐

☐   ☐

Financial/Real Estate Strategy Focus

What financial and/or real estate investment strategy will you focus on this quarter?

☐

☐

The 4 REI Freedoms: ☐ Time Freedom   ☐ Location Freedom

☐ Financial Freedom   ☐ Thought Freedom

ACTION TAKER QUARTERLY PLAN

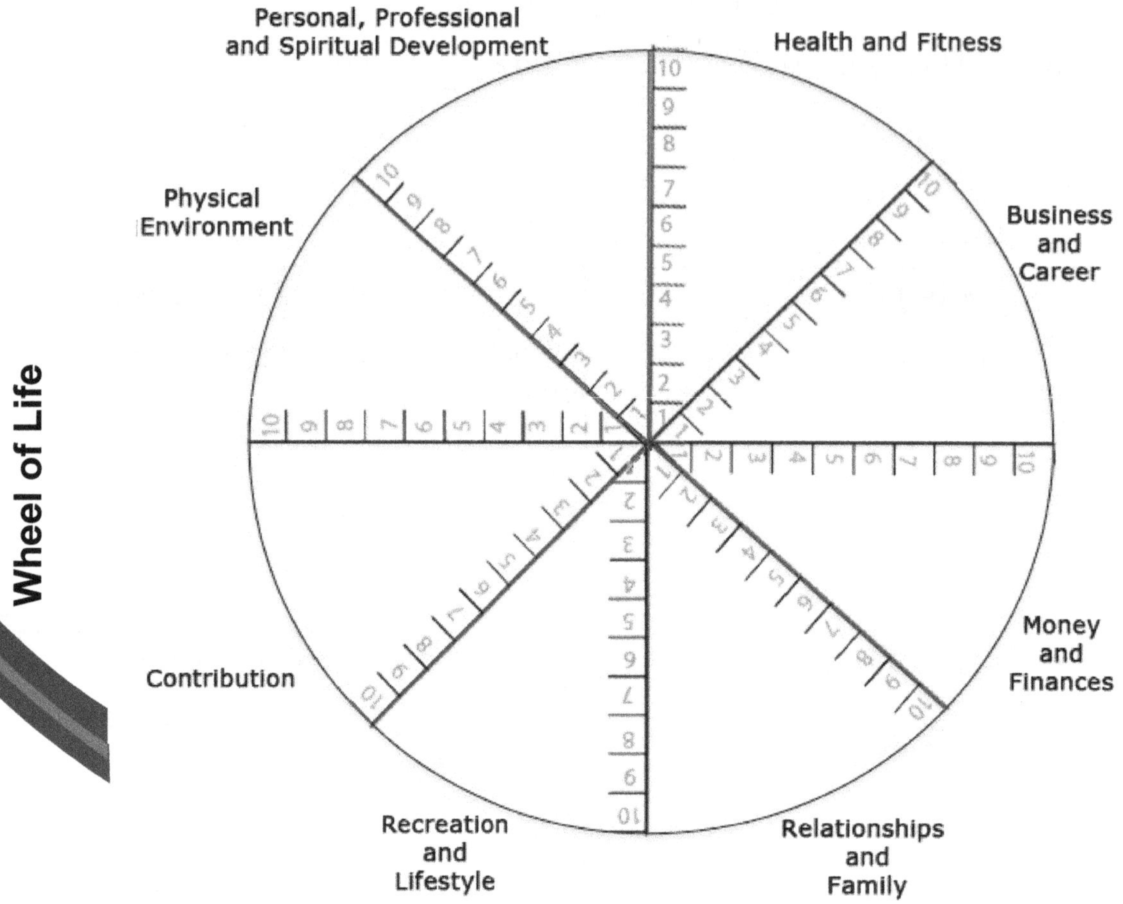
Wheel of Life
Personal, Professional and Spiritual Development
Health and Fitness
Business and Career
Money and Finances
Relationships and Family
Recreation and Lifestyle
Contribution
Physical Environment

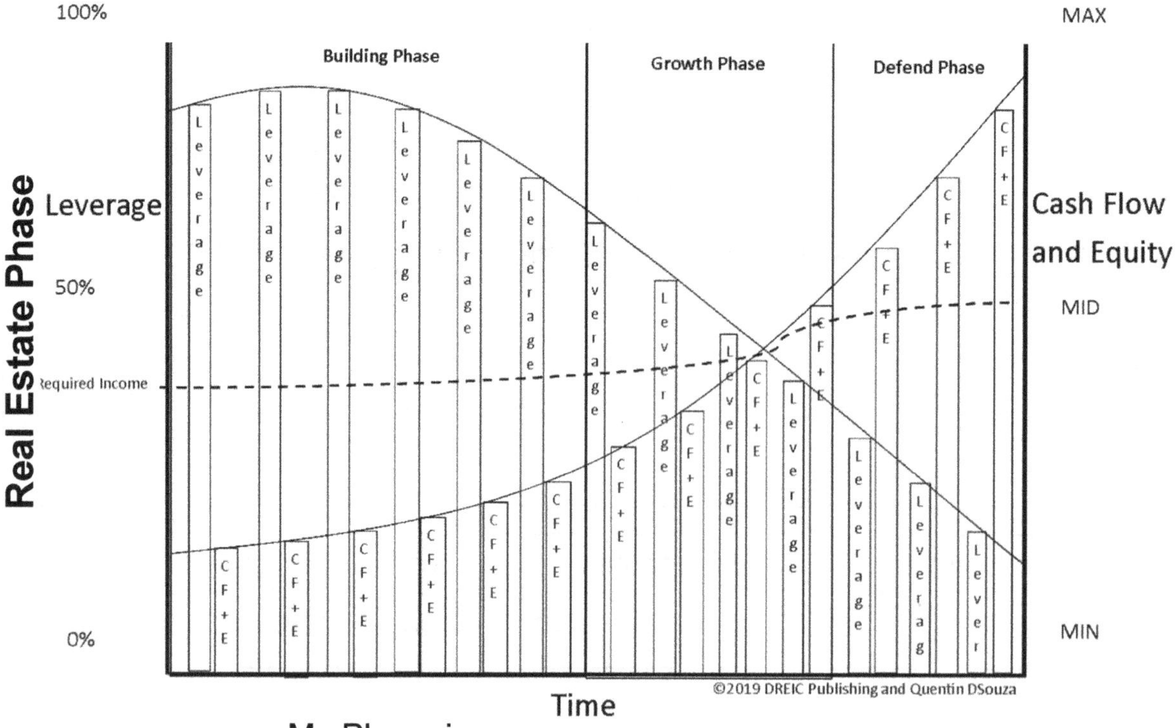
Real Estate Phase
100%
50%
0%
Leverage
Required Income
Building Phase
Growth Phase
Defend Phase
MAX
MID
MIN
Cash Flow and Equity
Time
©2019 DREIC Publishing and Quentin DSouza

My Phase is: ______________________

BALANCE SHEET

ASSETS		LIABILITIES	
Total Deposits:		Unsecured LOC:	
Unregistered Investments:		Car and Personal Loans:	
Registered Investments:		Secured Lines of Credit:	
Real Estate Portfolio:		Mortgages:	
Personal Assets:		Other:	
Other:			
Total Assets		Total Liabilities:	
Total Assets -Total Liabilities = **Net Worth:**			

☐ **High Net Worth Canadians**($1M-$5M) ☐ **Mid-Tier Millionaires**($5M-$30M) ☐ **Ultra High Net Worth**($30M+)

INCOME DIVERSITY

1. Salary/Hourly/Commission $_____

2. Real Estate Cash Flow After Expenses $_____

3. Business Profits $_____

4. Intellectual Property Residuals $_____

5. Interest Income $_____

6. Pensions, Benefits, Insurance $_____

7. Dividend Earnings/Options $_____

8. Sale of Assets $_____

9. Private Equity Yield $_____

10. Refinances $_____

11. Other Income $_____

TOTAL $_____

Date: _____   **Quarterly Plan for Real Estate Action Takers**

Three Areas of Focus This Quarter

Focus #1: _____

Result: _____

Actions Needed to Get the Result:

☐

☐

☐

Focus #2: _____

Result: _____

Actions Needed to Get the Result:

☐

☐

☐

Focus #3: _____

Result: _____

Actions Needed to Get the Result:

☐

☐

☐

Consistent growth in these three areas helps your real estate portfolio grow:

Finding	**Funding**	**Financing**
☐	☐	☐
☐	☐	☐

Quarter Starts: _____ **Quarter Ends:** _____

Quarterly Challenge

What challenge will take you out of your comfort zone this quarter?

☐

Delegate

What task(s) will you delegate this quarter?

☐

☐

Systems and Processes

What task(s) will you systematize this quarter?

☐

☐

Personal Development

What will you learn this quarter?

☐

☐

☐

Centers of Influence

Who will help you with your three areas of focus this quarter?

☐   ☐

☐   ☐

☐   ☐

Financial/Real Estate Strategy Focus

What financial and/or real estate investment strategy will you focus on this quarter?

☐

☐

The 4 REI Freedoms:	☐ Time Freedom	☐ Location Freedom
	☐ Financial Freedom	☐ Thought Freedom

ACTION TAKER QUARTERLY PLAN

Wheel of Life

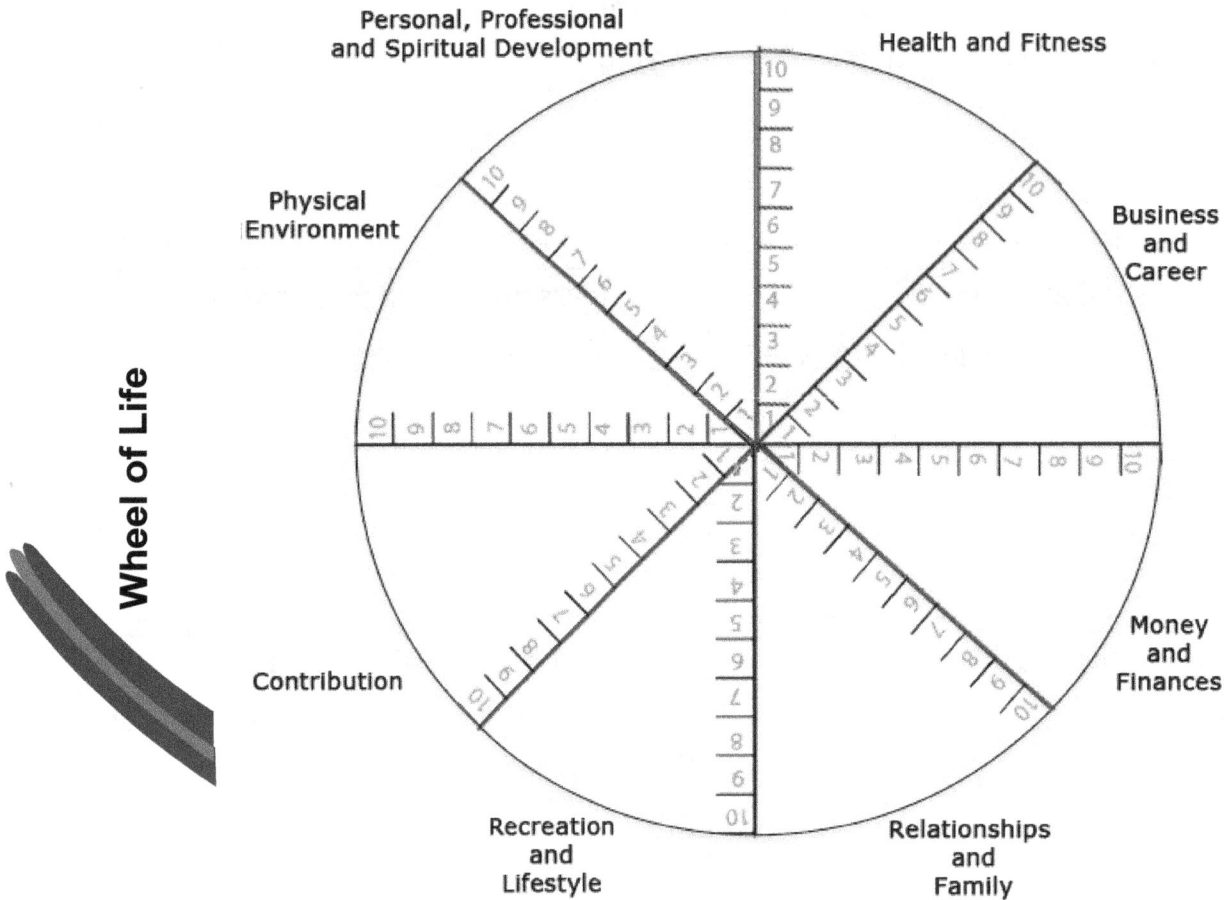

The Wheel of Life diagram with the following labeled segments:
- Personal, Professional and Spiritual Development
- Health and Fitness
- Physical Environment
- Business and Career
- Money and Finances
- Relationships and Family
- Recreation and Lifestyle
- Contribution

Real Estate Phase

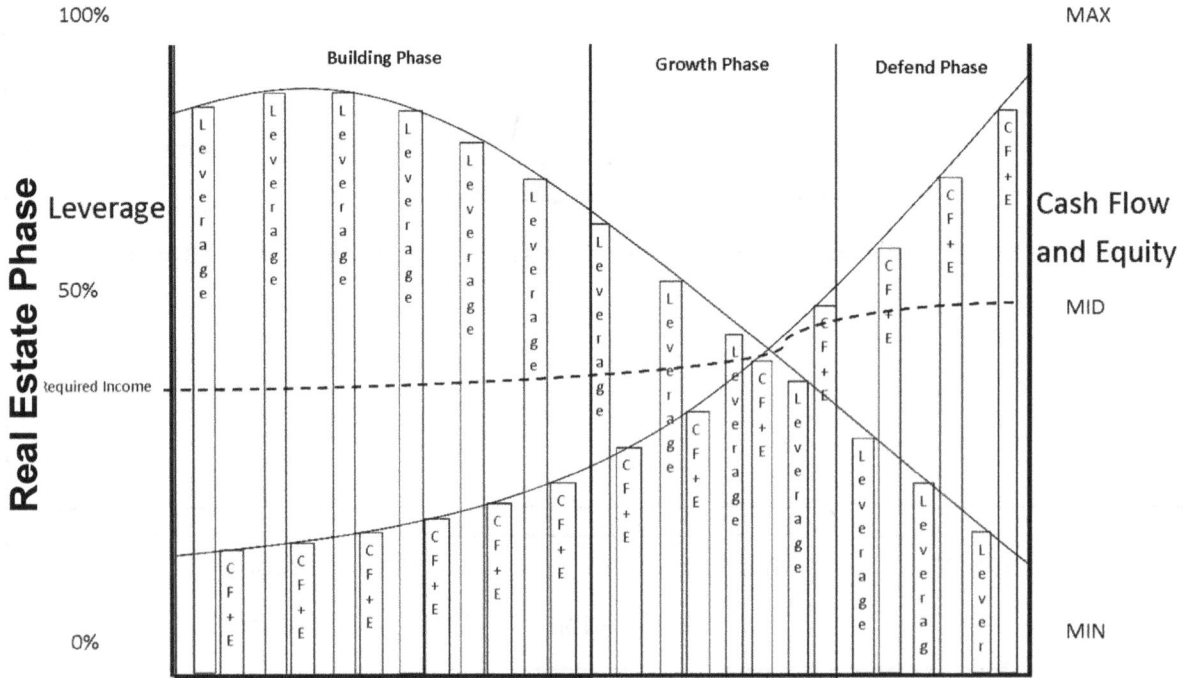

Chart showing Leverage vs Cash Flow and Equity over Time with:
- Building Phase
- Growth Phase
- Defend Phase

Left axis: 100%, 50%, Required Income, 0%
Right axis: MAX, MID, MIN

©2019 DREIC Publishing and Quentin DSouza

My Phase is: _____

BALANCE SHEET

ASSETS		LIABILITIES	
Total Deposits:		Unsecured LOC:	
Unregistered Investments:		Car and Personal Loans:	
Registered Investments:		Secured Lines of Credit:	
Real Estate Portfolio:		Mortgages:	
Personal Assets:		Other:	
Other:			
Total Assets		Total Liabilities:	
Total Assets -Total Liabilities = **Net Worth:**			

☐ **High Net Worth Canadians**($1M-$5M) ☐ **Mid-Tier Millionaires**($5M-$30M) ☐ **Ultra High Net Worth**($30M+)

INCOME DIVERSITY

1. Salary/Hourly/Commission $_____
2. Real Estate Cash Flow After Expenses $_____
3. Business Profits $_____
4. Intellectual Property Residuals $_____
5. Interest Income $_____
6. Pensions, Benefits, Insurance $_____
7. Dividend Earnings/Options $_____
8. Sale of Assets $_____
9. Private Equity Yield $_____
10. Refinances $_____
11. Other Income $_____

TOTAL $_____

Date: _____   **Quarterly Plan for Real Estate Action Takers**

Three Areas of Focus This Quarter

Focus #1: _____

Result: _____

Actions Needed to Get the Result:

☐

☐

☐

Focus #2: _____

Result: _____

Actions Needed to Get the Result:

☐

☐

☐

Focus #3: _____

Result: _____

Actions Needed to Get the Result:

☐

☐

☐

Consistent growth in these three areas helps your real estate portfolio grow:

Finding	**Funding**	**Financing**
☐	☐	☐
☐	☐	☐

Quarter Starts: _____ **Quarter Ends:** _____

Quarterly Challenge

What challenge will take you out of your comfort zone this quarter?

☐

Delegate	Systems and Processes
Delegate	**Systems and Processes**

Delegate

What task(s) will you delegate this quarter?

☐

☐

Systems and Processes

What task(s) will you systematize this quarter?

☐

☐

Personal Development

What will you learn this quarter?

☐

☐

☐

Centers of Influence

Who will help you with your three areas of focus this quarter?

☐ ☐

☐ ☐

☐ ☐

Financial/Real Estate Strategy Focus

What financial and/or real estate investment strategy will you focus on this quarter?

☐

☐

The 4 REI Freedoms: ☐ Time Freedom ☐ Location Freedom
☐ Financial Freedom ☐ Thought Freedom

ACTION TAKER QUARTERLY PLAN

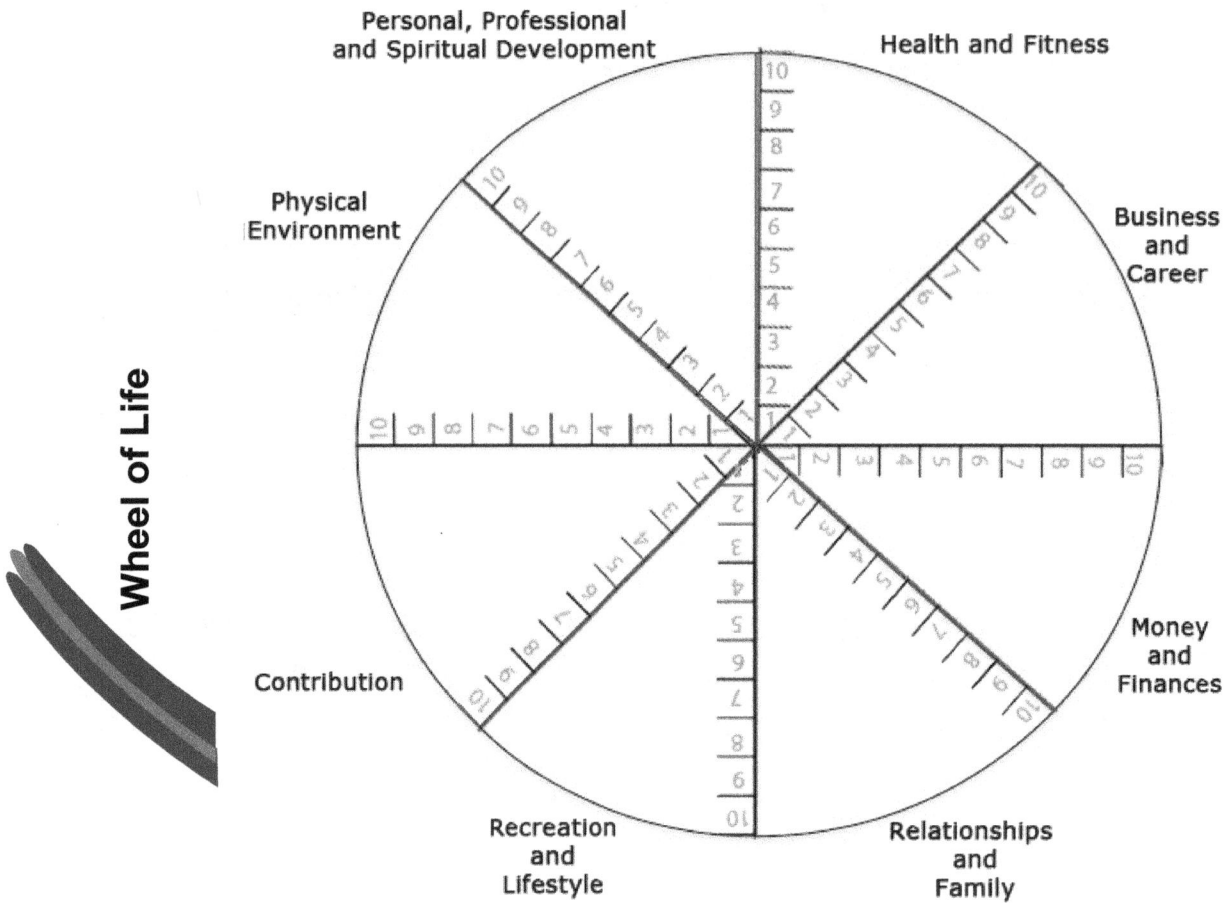

Wheel of Life

Personal, Professional and Spiritual Development

Health and Fitness

Physical Environment

Business and Career

Contribution

Money and Finances

Recreation and Lifestyle

Relationships and Family

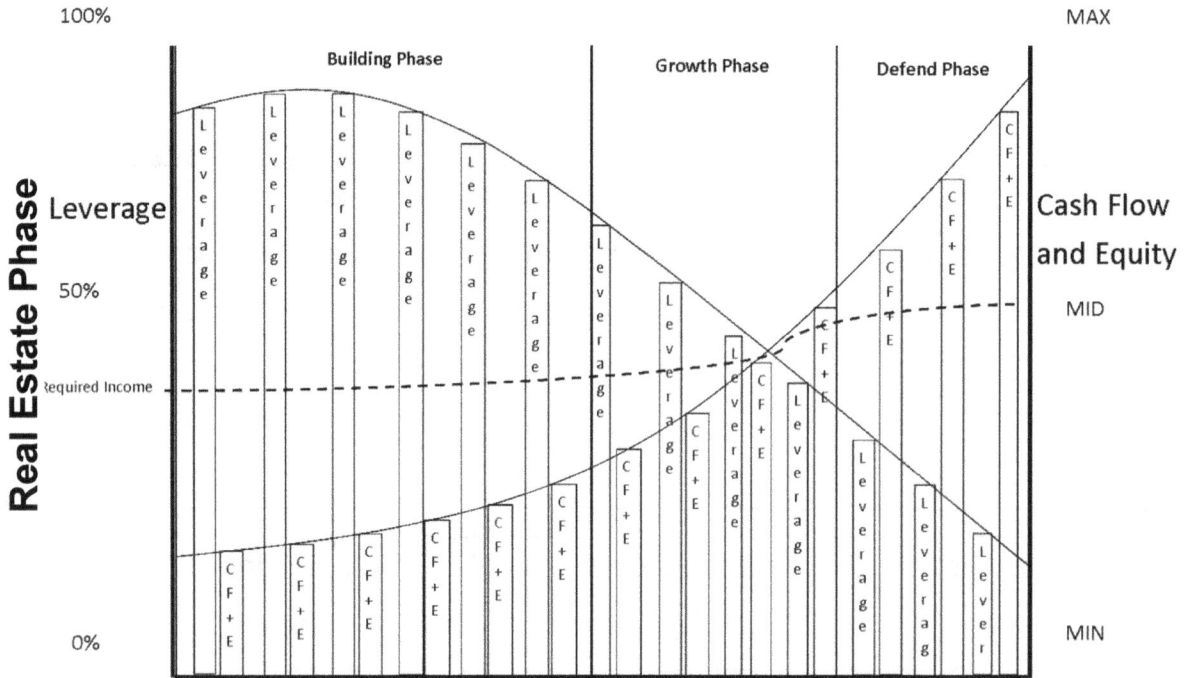

Real Estate Phase

Building Phase

Growth Phase

Defend Phase

100%

MAX

Leverage

Cash Flow and Equity

50%

MID

Required Income

0%

MIN

Time

©2019 DREIC Publishing and Quentin DSouza

My Phase is: _____

BALANCE SHEET

ASSETS		LIABILITIES	
Total Deposits:		Unsecured LOC:	
Unregistered Investments:		Car and Personal Loans:	
Registered Investments:		Secured Lines of Credit:	
Real Estate Portfolio:		Mortgages:	
Personal Assets:		Other:	
Other:			
Total Assets		Total Liabilities:	
Total Assets -Total Liabilities = **Net Worth:**			

☐ **High Net Worth Canadians**($1M-$5M) ☐ **Mid-Tier Millionaires**($5M-$30M) ☐ **Ultra High Net Worth**($30M+)

INCOME DIVERSITY

1. Salary/Hourly/Commission	$_____
2. Real Estate Cash Flow After Expenses	$_____
3. Business Profits	$_____
4. Intellectual Property Residuals	$_____
5. Interest Income	$_____
6. Pensions, Benefits, Insurance	$_____
7. Dividend Earnings/Options	$_____
8. Sale of Assets	$_____
9. Private Equity Yield	$_____
10. Refinances	$_____
11. Other Income	$_____
TOTAL	$_____

Date: _____   **Quarterly Plan for Real Estate Action Takers**

Three Areas of Focus This Quarter

Focus #1: _____

Result: _____

Actions Needed to Get the Result:

☐

☐

☐

Focus #2: _____

Result: _____

Actions Needed to Get the Result:

☐

☐

☐

Focus #3: _____

Result: _____

Actions Needed to Get the Result:

☐

☐

☐

Consistent growth in these three areas helps your real estate portfolio grow:

Finding	Funding	Financing
☐	☐	☐
☐	☐	☐

Quarter Starts: _____ **Quarter Ends:** _____

Quarterly Challenge

What challenge will take you out of your comfort zone this quarter?

☐

Delegate

What task(s) will you delegate this quarter?

☐

☐

Systems and Processes

What task(s) will you systematize this quarter?

☐

☐

Personal Development

What will you learn this quarter?

☐

☐

☐

Centers of Influence

Who will help you with your three areas of focus this quarter?

☐   ☐

☐   ☐

☐   ☐

Financial/Real Estate Strategy Focus

What financial and/or real estate investment strategy will you focus on this quarter?

☐

☐

The 4 REI Freedoms: ☐ Time Freedom   ☐ Location Freedom

☐ Financial Freedom   ☐ Thought Freedom

ACTION TAKER QUARTERLY PLAN

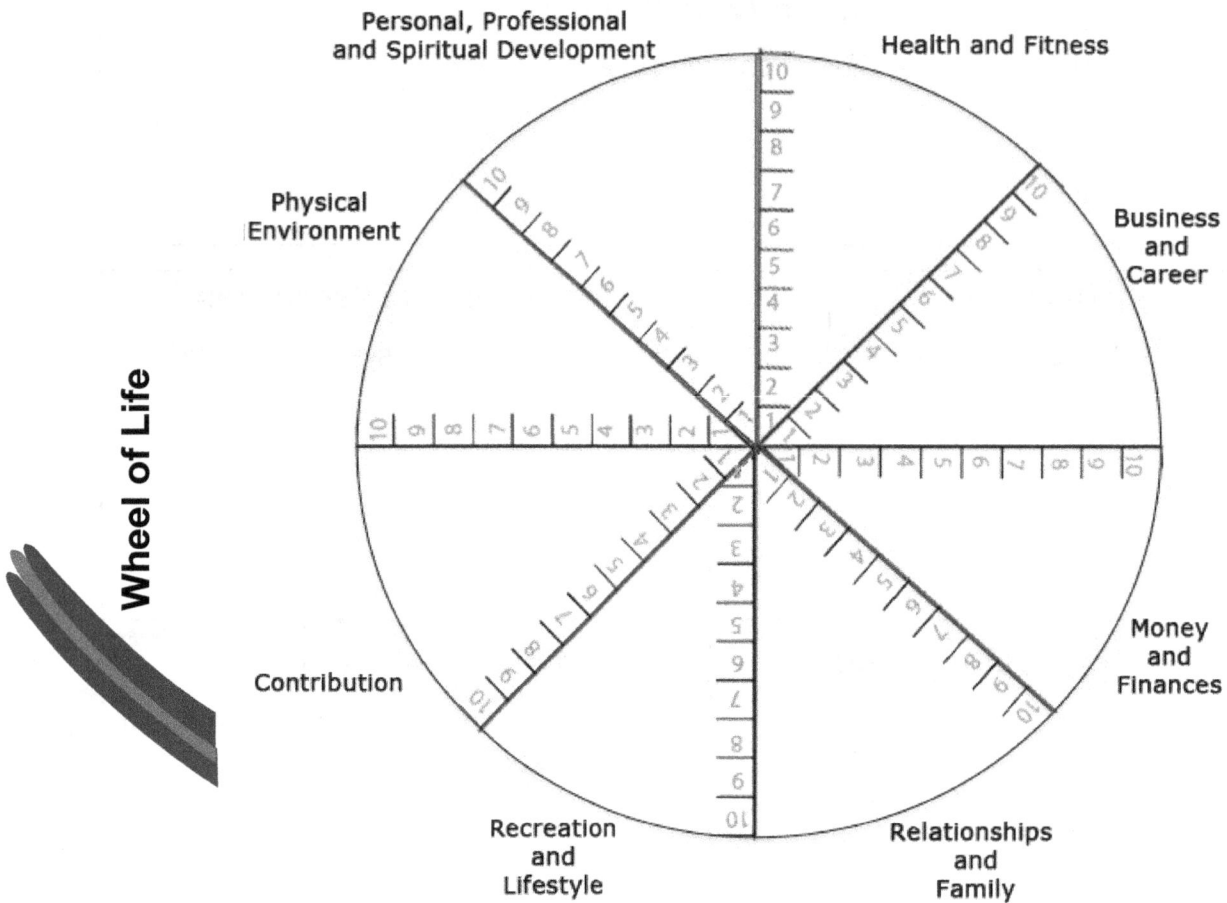

Wheel of Life

Personal, Professional and Spiritual Development
Health and Fitness
Physical Environment
Business and Career
Contribution
Money and Finances
Recreation and Lifestyle
Relationships and Family

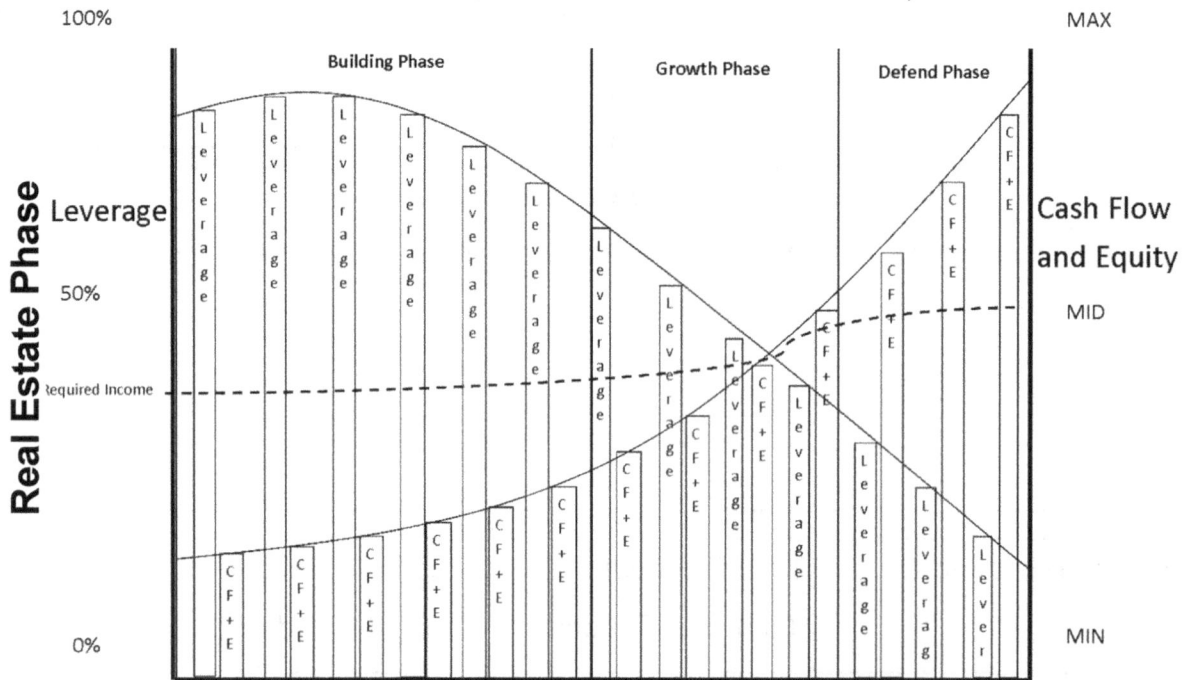

Real Estate Phase

Building Phase — Growth Phase — Defend Phase

Leverage

Cash Flow and Equity

Required Income

©2019 DREIC Publishing and Quentin DSouza

Time

My Phase is: _____

CHAPTER 6

Weekly Plan Template

Weekly Plan for Real Estate Action Takers

☐ **Monday**	☐ **Tuesday**	☐ **Wednesday**
Priority:_____	Priority:_____	Priority:_____
6 _____	6 _____	6 _____
7 _____	7 _____	7 _____
8 _____	8 _____	8 _____
9 _____	9 _____	9 _____
10 _____	10 _____	10 _____
11 _____	11 _____	11 _____
12 _____	12 _____	12 _____
1 _____	1 _____	1 _____
2 _____	2 _____	2 _____
3 _____	3 _____	3 _____
4 _____	4 _____	4 _____
5 _____	5 _____	5 _____
6 _____	6 _____	6 _____
7 _____	7 _____	7 _____
8 _____	8 _____	8 _____
9 _____	9 _____	9 _____
10 _____	10 _____	10 _____

Three Priorities This Week

Getting these done will make an awesome week.

☐

☐

☐

Quarterly Plan

These actions move your quarterly plan forward.

☐

☐

☐

Eat That Frog

What have you been procrastinating on?

☐

Week Starts: _____ **Week Ends:** _____ **Quarter Ends:** _____

Thursday
Priority: _____
6 _____
7 _____
8 _____
9 _____
10 _____
11 _____
12 _____
1 _____
2 _____
3 _____
4 _____
5 _____
6 _____
7 _____
8 _____
9 _____
10 _____

Friday
Priority: _____
6 _____
7 _____
8 _____
9 _____
10 _____
11 _____
12 _____
1 _____
2 _____
3 _____
4 _____
5 _____
6 _____
7 _____
8 _____
9 _____
10 _____

Saturday
_____
_____
_____
_____
_____
_____
_____

Sunday
_____
_____
_____
_____
_____
_____
_____

Finding	**Funding**	**Financing**
Actions this week to find new properties: ☐	Actions this week to access credit, investors or cash: ☐	Actions this week to access private lenders or financing: ☐
Do, Delegate, Dump	**Celebrate Life**	**Centers of Influence**
Actions this week working on your business: ☐	Fun actions this week that focus on the present. ☐	Actions to develop these relationships: ☐

Accountability Call   ☐ Next Call Scheduled   ☐ Completed

Weekly Plan for Real Estate Action Takers

☐ **Monday**	☐ **Tuesday**	☐ **Wednesday**
Priority:_____	Priority:_____	Priority:_____
6 _____	6 _____	6 _____
7 _____	7 _____	7 _____
8 _____	8 _____	8 _____
9 _____	9 _____	9 _____
10 _____	10 _____	10 _____
11 _____	11 _____	11 _____
12 _____	12 _____	12 _____
1 _____	1 _____	1 _____
2 _____	2 _____	2 _____
3 _____	3 _____	3 _____
4 _____	4 _____	4 _____
5 _____	5 _____	5 _____
6 _____	6 _____	6 _____
7 _____	7 _____	7 _____
8 _____	8 _____	8 _____
9 _____	9 _____	9 _____
10 _____	10 _____	10 _____

Three Priorities This Week

Getting these done will make an awesome week.

☐

☐

☐

Quarterly Plan

These actions move your quarterly plan forward.

☐

☐

☐

Eat That Frog

What have you been procrastinating on?

☐

Week Starts: _____ **Week Ends:** _____ **Quarter Ends:** _____

☐ **Thursday**	☐ **Friday**	☐ **Saturday**
Priority:_____	Priority:_____	_____
6 _____	6 _____	_____
7 _____	7 _____	_____
8 _____	8 _____	_____
9 _____	9 _____	_____
10 _____	10 _____	_____
11 _____	11 _____	_____
12 _____	12 _____	_____
1 _____	1 _____	☐ **Sunday**
2 _____	2 _____	
3 _____	3 _____	_____
4 _____	4 _____	_____
5 _____	5 _____	_____
6 _____	6 _____	_____
7 _____	7 _____	_____
8 _____	8 _____	_____
9 _____	9 _____	_____
10 _____	10 _____	_____

Finding	**Funding**	**Financing**
Actions this week to find new properties: ☐	Actions this week to access credit, investors or cash: ☐	Actions this week to access private lenders or financing: ☐
Do, Delegate, Dump	**Celebrate Life**	**Centers of Influence**
Actions this week working on your business: ☐	Fun actions this week that focus on the present. ☐	Actions to develop these relationships: ☐

Accountability Call   ☐ Next Call Scheduled   ☐ Completed

Weekly Plan for Real Estate Action Takers

☐ **Monday**	☐ **Tuesday**	☐ **Wednesday**
Priority:_____	Priority:_____	Priority:_____
6 _____	6 _____	6 _____
7 _____	7 _____	7 _____
8 _____	8 _____	8 _____
9 _____	9 _____	9 _____
10 _____	10 _____	10 _____
11 _____	11 _____	11 _____
12 _____	12 _____	12 _____
1 _____	1 _____	1 _____
2 _____	2 _____	2 _____
3 _____	3 _____	3 _____
4 _____	4 _____	4 _____
5 _____	5 _____	5 _____
6 _____	6 _____	6 _____
7 _____	7 _____	7 _____
8 _____	8 _____	8 _____
9 _____	9 _____	9 _____
10 _____	10 _____	10 _____

Three Priorities This Week

Getting these done will make an awesome week.

☐

☐

☐

Quarterly Plan

These actions move your quarterly plan forward.

☐

☐

☐

Eat That Frog

What have you been procrastinating on?

☐

Week Starts: _____ Week Ends: _____ Quarter Ends: _____

	Thursday		Friday		Saturday

Thursday

Priority:_____

6 _____
7 _____
8 _____
9 _____
10 _____
11 _____
12 _____
1 _____
2 _____
3 _____
4 _____
5 _____
6 _____
7 _____
8 _____
9 _____
10 _____

Friday

Priority:_____

6 _____
7 _____
8 _____
9 _____
10 _____
11 _____
12 _____
1 _____
2 _____
3 _____
4 _____
5 _____
6 _____
7 _____
8 _____
9 _____
10 _____

Saturday

_____
_____
_____
_____
_____
_____
_____

Sunday

_____
_____
_____
_____
_____
_____
_____

Finding	Funding	Financing
Actions this week to find new properties: ☐	Actions this week to access credit, investors or cash: ☐	Actions this week to access private lenders or financing: ☐
Do, Delegate, Dump	**Celebrate Life**	**Centers of Influence**
Actions this week working on your business: ☐	Fun actions this week that focus on the present. ☐	Actions to develop these relationships: ☐

Accountability Call   ☐ Next Call Scheduled   ☐ Completed

Weekly Plan for Real Estate Action Takers

☐ **Monday**	☐ **Tuesday**	☐ **Wednesday**
Priority:_____	Priority:_____	Priority:_____
6 _____	6 _____	6 _____
7 _____	7 _____	7 _____
8 _____	8 _____	8 _____
9 _____	9 _____	9 _____
10 _____	10 _____	10 _____
11 _____	11 _____	11 _____
12 _____	12 _____	12 _____
1 _____	1 _____	1 _____
2 _____	2 _____	2 _____
3 _____	3 _____	3 _____
4 _____	4 _____	4 _____
5 _____	5 _____	5 _____
6 _____	6 _____	6 _____
7 _____	7 _____	7 _____
8 _____	8 _____	8 _____
9 _____	9 _____	9 _____
10 _____	10 _____	10 _____

Three Priorities This Week

Getting these done will make an awesome week.

☐

☐

☐

Quarterly Plan

These actions move your quarterly plan forward.

☐

☐

☐

Eat That Frog

What have you been procrastinating on?

☐

Week Starts: _____ **Week Ends:** _____ **Quarter Ends:** _____

☐ **Thursday**	☐ **Friday**	☐ **Saturday**
Priority:_____	Priority:_____	_____
6 _____	6 _____	_____
7 _____	7 _____	_____
8 _____	8 _____	_____
9 _____	9 _____	_____
10 _____	10 _____	_____
11 _____	11 _____	_____
12 _____	12 _____	_____
1 _____	1 _____	
2 _____	2 _____	☐ **Sunday**
3 _____	3 _____	_____
4 _____	4 _____	_____
5 _____	5 _____	_____
6 _____	6 _____	_____
7 _____	7 _____	_____
8 _____	8 _____	_____
9 _____	9 _____	_____
10 _____	10 _____	_____

Finding	**Funding**	**Financing**
Actions this week to find new properties: ☐	Actions this week to access credit, investors or cash: ☐	Actions this week to access private lenders or financing: ☐
Do, Delegate, Dump	**Celebrate Life**	**Centers of Influence**
Actions this week working on your business: ☐	Fun actions this week that focus on the present. ☐	Actions to develop these relationships: ☐

Accountability Call　☐ Next Call Scheduled　　☐ Completed

Weekly Plan for Real Estate Action Takers

Monday	Tuesday	Wednesday
Priority:_____	Priority:_____	Priority:_____
6 _____	6 _____	6 _____
7 _____	7 _____	7 _____
8 _____	8 _____	8 _____
9 _____	9 _____	9 _____
10 _____	10 _____	10 _____
11 _____	11 _____	11 _____
12 _____	12 _____	12 _____
1 _____	1 _____	1 _____
2 _____	2 _____	2 _____
3 _____	3 _____	3 _____
4 _____	4 _____	4 _____
5 _____	5 _____	5 _____
6 _____	6 _____	6 _____
7 _____	7 _____	7 _____
8 _____	8 _____	8 _____
9 _____	9 _____	9 _____
10 _____	10 _____	10 _____

Three Priorities This Week

Getting these done will make an awesome week.

☐

☐

☐

Quarterly Plan

These actions move your quarterly plan forward.

☐

☐

☐

Eat That Frog

What have you been procrastinating on?

☐

Week Starts: _____ Week Ends: _____ Quarter Ends: _____

Thursday	Friday	Saturday
Priority:_____	Priority:_____	
6 _____	6 _____	
7 _____	7 _____	
8 _____	8 _____	
9 _____	9 _____	
10 _____	10 _____	
11 _____	11 _____	
12 _____	12 _____	
1 _____	1 _____	
2 _____	2 _____	**Sunday**
3 _____	3 _____	
4 _____	4 _____	
5 _____	5 _____	
6 _____	6 _____	
7 _____	7 _____	
8 _____	8 _____	
9 _____	9 _____	
10 _____	10 _____	

Finding	Funding	Financing
Actions this week to find new properties: ☐	Actions this week to access credit, investors or cash: ☐	Actions this week to access private lenders or financing: ☐
Do, Delegate, Dump	**Celebrate Life**	**Centers of Influence**
Actions this week working on your business: ☐	Fun actions this week that focus on the present. ☐	Actions to develop these relationships: ☐

Accountability Call   ☐ Next Call Scheduled   ☐ Completed

Weekly Plan for Real Estate Action Takers

	Monday		Tuesday		Wednesday

Priority: _____

Priority: _____

Priority: _____

Monday:
6 _____
7 _____
8 _____
9 _____
10 _____
11 _____
12 _____
1 _____
2 _____
3 _____
4 _____
5 _____
6 _____
7 _____
8 _____
9 _____
10 _____

Tuesday:
6 _____
7 _____
8 _____
9 _____
10 _____
11 _____
12 _____
1 _____
2 _____
3 _____
4 _____
5 _____
6 _____
7 _____
8 _____
9 _____
10 _____

Wednesday:
6 _____
7 _____
8 _____
9 _____
10 _____
11 _____
12 _____
1 _____
2 _____
3 _____
4 _____
5 _____
6 _____
7 _____
8 _____
9 _____
10 _____

Three Priorities This Week

Getting these done will make an awesome week.

☐

☐

☐

Quarterly Plan

These actions move your quarterly plan forward.

☐

☐

☐

Eat That Frog

What have you been procrastinating on?

☐

Week Starts: _____ **Week Ends:** _____ **Quarter Ends:** _____

☐ **Thursday**	☐ **Friday**	☐ **Saturday**
Priority:_____	Priority:_____	
6 _____	6 _____	_____
7 _____	7 _____	_____
8 _____	8 _____	_____
9 _____	9 _____	_____
10 _____	10 _____	_____
11 _____	11 _____	_____
12 _____	12 _____	_____
1 _____	1 _____	
2 _____	2 _____	☐ **Sunday**
3 _____	3 _____	
4 _____	4 _____	_____
5 _____	5 _____	_____
6 _____	6 _____	_____
7 _____	7 _____	_____
8 _____	8 _____	_____
9 _____	9 _____	_____
10 _____	10 _____	_____

Finding	**Funding**	**Financing**
Actions this week to find new properties: ☐	Actions this week to access credit, investors or cash: ☐	Actions this week to access private lenders or financing: ☐
Do, Delegate, Dump	**Celebrate Life**	**Centers of Influence**
Actions this week working on your business: ☐	Fun actions this week that focus on the present. ☐	Actions to develop these relationships: ☐
Accountability Call ☐ Next Call Scheduled ☐ Completed		

Monday	**Tuesday**	**Wednesday**
Priority:_____	Priority:_____	Priority:_____
6 _____	6 _____	6 _____
7 _____	7 _____	7 _____
8 _____	8 _____	8 _____
9 _____	9 _____	9 _____
10 _____	10 _____	10 _____
11 _____	11 _____	11 _____
12 _____	12 _____	12 _____
1 _____	1 _____	1 _____
2 _____	2 _____	2 _____
3 _____	3 _____	3 _____
4 _____	4 _____	4 _____
5 _____	5 _____	5 _____
6 _____	6 _____	6 _____
7 _____	7 _____	7 _____
8 _____	8 _____	8 _____
9 _____	9 _____	9 _____
10 _____	10 _____	10 _____

Three Priorities This Week

Getting these done will make an awesome week.

☐

☐

☐

Quarterly Plan

These actions move your quarterly plan forward.

☐

☐

☐

Eat That Frog

What have you been procrastinating on?

☐

Week Starts: _____ **Week Ends:** _____ **Quarter Ends:** _____

☐ **Thursday**	☐ **Friday**	☐ **Saturday**

Thursday

Priority:_____

6 _____
7 _____
8 _____
9 _____
10 _____
11 _____
12 _____
1 _____
2 _____
3 _____
4 _____
5 _____
6 _____
7 _____
8 _____
9 _____
10 _____

Friday

Priority:_____

6 _____
7 _____
8 _____
9 _____
10 _____
11 _____
12 _____
1 _____
2 _____
3 _____
4 _____
5 _____
6 _____
7 _____
8 _____
9 _____
10 _____

Saturday

_____
_____
_____
_____
_____
_____
_____

☐ **Sunday**

_____
_____
_____
_____
_____
_____

Finding	**Funding**	**Financing**
Actions this week to find new properties: ☐	Actions this week to access credit, investors or cash: ☐	Actions this week to access private lenders or financing: ☐
Do, Delegate, Dump	**Celebrate Life**	**Centers of Influence**
Actions this week working on your business: ☐	Fun actions this week that focus on the present. ☐	Actions to develop these relationships: ☐
Accountability Call ☐ Next Call Scheduled ☐ Completed		

Weekly Plan for Real Estate Action Takers

Monday

Priority:_____

6 _____
7 _____
8 _____
9 _____
10 _____
11 _____
12 _____
1 _____
2 _____
3 _____
4 _____
5 _____
6 _____
7 _____
8 _____
9 _____
10 _____

Tuesday

Priority:_____

6 _____
7 _____
8 _____
9 _____
10 _____
11 _____
12 _____
1 _____
2 _____
3 _____
4 _____
5 _____
6 _____
7 _____
8 _____
9 _____
10 _____

Wednesday

Priority:_____

6 _____
7 _____
8 _____
9 _____
10 _____
11 _____
12 _____
1 _____
2 _____
3 _____
4 _____
5 _____
6 _____
7 _____
8 _____
9 _____
10 _____

Three Priorities This Week

Getting these done will make an awesome week.

☐

☐

☐

Quarterly Plan

These actions move your quarterly plan forward.

☐

☐

☐

Eat That Frog

What have you been procrastinating on?

☐

Week Starts: _____ **Week Ends:** _____ **Quarter Ends:** _____

☐ Thursday

Priority:_____

6 _____
7 _____
8 _____
9 _____
10 _____
11 _____
12 _____
1 _____
2 _____
3 _____
4 _____
5 _____
6 _____
7 _____
8 _____
9 _____
10 _____

☐ Friday

Priority:_____

6 _____
7 _____
8 _____
9 _____
10 _____
11 _____
12 _____
1 _____
2 _____
3 _____
4 _____
5 _____
6 _____
7 _____
8 _____
9 _____
10 _____

☐ Saturday

_____
_____
_____
_____
_____
_____
_____

☐ Sunday

_____
_____
_____
_____
_____
_____
_____

Finding	**Funding**	**Financing**
Actions this week to find new properties: ☐	Actions this week to access credit, investors or cash: ☐	Actions this week to access private lenders or financing: ☐
Do, Delegate, Dump	**Celebrate Life**	**Centers of Influence**
Actions this week working on your business: ☐	Fun actions this week that focus on the present. ☐	Actions to develop these relationships: ☐

Accountability Call   ☐ Next Call Scheduled   ☐ Completed

☐ **Monday**	☐ **Tuesday**	☐ **Wednesday**
Priority:_____	Priority:_____	Priority:_____
6 _____	6 _____	6 _____
7 _____	7 _____	7 _____
8 _____	8 _____	8 _____
9 _____	9 _____	9 _____
10 _____	10 _____	10 _____
11 _____	11 _____	11 _____
12 _____	12 _____	12 _____
1 _____	1 _____	1 _____
2 _____	2 _____	2 _____
3 _____	3 _____	3 _____
4 _____	4 _____	4 _____
5 _____	5 _____	5 _____
6 _____	6 _____	6 _____
7 _____	7 _____	7 _____
8 _____	8 _____	8 _____
9 _____	9 _____	9 _____
10 _____	10 _____	10 _____

Three Priorities This Week

Getting these done will make an awesome week.

☐

☐

☐

Quarterly Plan

These actions move your quarterly plan forward.

☐

☐

☐

Eat That Frog

What have you been procrastinating on?

☐

Week Starts: _____ Week Ends: _____ Quarter Ends: _____

☐ **Thursday**	☐ **Friday**	☐ **Saturday**
Priority:_____	Priority:_____	_____
6 _____	6 _____	_____
7 _____	7 _____	_____
8 _____	8 _____	_____
9 _____	9 _____	_____
10 _____	10 _____	_____
11 _____	11 _____	_____
12 _____	12 _____	_____
1 _____	1 _____	_____
2 _____	2 _____	☐ **Sunday**
3 _____	3 _____	_____
4 _____	4 _____	_____
5 _____	5 _____	_____
6 _____	6 _____	_____
7 _____	7 _____	_____
8 _____	8 _____	_____
9 _____	9 _____	_____
10 _____	10 _____	_____

Finding	**Funding**	**Financing**
Actions this week to find new properties: ☐	Actions this week to access credit, investors or cash: ☐	Actions this week to access private lenders or financing: ☐
Do, Delegate, Dump	**Celebrate Life**	**Centers of Influence**
Actions this week working on your business: ☐	Fun actions this week that focus on the present. ☐	Actions to develop these relationships: ☐
Accountability Call ☐ Next Call Scheduled ☐ Completed		

Weekly Plan for Real Estate Action Takers

	Monday		**Tuesday**		**Wednesday**
Priority:_____		Priority:_____		Priority:_____	

Monday	Tuesday	Wednesday
6 _____	6 _____	6 _____
7 _____	7 _____	7 _____
8 _____	8 _____	8 _____
9 _____	9 _____	9 _____
10 _____	10 _____	10 _____
11 _____	11 _____	11 _____
12 _____	12 _____	12 _____
1 _____	1 _____	1 _____
2 _____	2 _____	2 _____
3 _____	3 _____	3 _____
4 _____	4 _____	4 _____
5 _____	5 _____	5 _____
6 _____	6 _____	6 _____
7 _____	7 _____	7 _____
8 _____	8 _____	8 _____
9 _____	9 _____	9 _____
10 _____	10 _____	10 _____

Three Priorities This Week

Getting these done will make an awesome week.

☐

☐

☐

Quarterly Plan

These actions move your quarterly plan forward.

☐

☐

☐

Eat That Frog

What have you been procrastinating on?

☐

Week Starts: _____ **Week Ends:** _____ **Quarter Ends:** _____

☐ **Thursday**	☐ **Friday**	☐ **Saturday**
Priority:_____	Priority:_____	
6 _____	6 _____	
7 _____	7 _____	
8 _____	8 _____	
9 _____	9 _____	
10 _____	10 _____	
11 _____	11 _____	
12 _____	12 _____	
1 _____	1 _____	☐ **Sunday**
2 _____	2 _____	
3 _____	3 _____	
4 _____	4 _____	
5 _____	5 _____	
6 _____	6 _____	
7 _____	7 _____	
8 _____	8 _____	
9 _____	9 _____	
10 _____	10 _____	

Finding	**Funding**	**Financing**
Actions this week to find new properties: ☐	Actions this week to access credit, investors or cash: ☐	Actions this week to access private lenders or financing: ☐
Do, Delegate, Dump	**Celebrate Life**	**Centers of Influence**
Actions this week working on your business: ☐	Fun actions this week that focus on the present. ☐	Actions to develop these relationships: ☐

Accountability Call   ☐ Next Call Scheduled   ☐ Completed

Weekly Plan for Real Estate Action Takers

☐ **Monday**	☐ **Tuesday**	☐ **Wednesday**
Priority:_____	Priority:_____	Priority:_____
6	6	6
7	7	7
8	8	8
9	9	9
10	10	10
11	11	11
12	12	12
1	1	1
2	2	2
3	3	3
4	4	4
5	5	5
6	6	6
7	7	7
8	8	8
9	9	9
10	10	10

Three Priorities This Week

Getting these done will make an awesome week.

☐

☐

☐

Quarterly Plan

These actions move your quarterly plan forward.

☐

☐

☐

Eat That Frog

What have you been procrastinating on?

☐

Week Starts: _____ **Week Ends:** _____ **Quarter Ends:** _____

☐ **Thursday**	☐ **Friday**	☐ **Saturday**

Thursday

Priority:_____

6 _____
7 _____
8 _____
9 _____
10 _____
11 _____
12 _____
1 _____
2 _____
3 _____
4 _____
5 _____
6 _____
7 _____
8 _____
9 _____
10 _____

Friday

Priority:_____

6 _____
7 _____
8 _____
9 _____
10 _____
11 _____
12 _____
1 _____
2 _____
3 _____
4 _____
5 _____
6 _____
7 _____
8 _____
9 _____
10 _____

Saturday

_____
_____
_____
_____
_____
_____
_____

☐ **Sunday**

_____
_____
_____
_____
_____
_____
_____

Finding	**Funding**	**Financing**
Actions this week to find new properties: ☐	Actions this week to access credit, investors or cash: ☐	Actions this week to access private lenders or financing: ☐
Do, Delegate, Dump	**Celebrate Life**	**Centers of Influence**
Actions this week working on your business: ☐	Fun actions this week that focus on the present. ☐	Actions to develop these relationships: ☐

Accountability Call   ☐ Next Call Scheduled   ☐ Completed

Weekly Plan for Real Estate Action Takers

Monday

Priority:_____

6 _____
7 _____
8 _____
9 _____
10 _____
11 _____
12 _____
1 _____
2 _____
3 _____
4 _____
5 _____
6 _____
7 _____
8 _____
9 _____
10 _____

Tuesday

Priority:_____

6 _____
7 _____
8 _____
9 _____
10 _____
11 _____
12 _____
1 _____
2 _____
3 _____
4 _____
5 _____
6 _____
7 _____
8 _____
9 _____
10 _____

Wednesday

Priority:_____

6 _____
7 _____
8 _____
9 _____
10 _____
11 _____
12 _____
1 _____
2 _____
3 _____
4 _____
5 _____
6 _____
7 _____
8 _____
9 _____
10 _____

Three Priorities This Week

Getting these done will make an awesome week.

☐

☐

☐

Quarterly Plan

These actions move your quarterly plan forward.

☐

☐

☐

Eat That Frog

What have you been procrastinating on?

☐

Week Starts: _____ **Week Ends:** _____ **Quarter Ends:** _____

☐ **Thursday**	☐ **Friday**	☐ **Saturday**
Priority:_____	Priority:_____	_____
6 _____	6 _____	_____
7 _____	7 _____	_____
8 _____	8 _____	_____
9 _____	9 _____	_____
10 _____	10 _____	_____
11 _____	11 _____	_____
12 _____	12 _____	_____
1 _____	1 _____	
2 _____	2 _____	☐ **Sunday**
3 _____	3 _____	_____
4 _____	4 _____	_____
5 _____	5 _____	_____
6 _____	6 _____	_____
7 _____	7 _____	_____
8 _____	8 _____	_____
9 _____	9 _____	_____
10 _____	10 _____	_____

Finding	**Funding**	**Financing**
Actions this week to find new properties: ☐	Actions this week to access credit, investors or cash: ☐	Actions this week to access private lenders or financing: ☐
Do, Delegate, Dump	**Celebrate Life**	**Centers of Influence**
Actions this week working on your business: ☐	Fun actions this week that focus on the present. ☐	Actions to develop these relationships: ☐

Accountability Call   ☐ Next Call Scheduled   ☐ Completed

Weekly Plan for Real Estate Action Takers

Monday

Priority:_____

6 _____
7 _____
8 _____
9 _____
10 _____
11 _____
12 _____
1 _____
2 _____
3 _____
4 _____
5 _____
6 _____
7 _____
8 _____
9 _____
10 _____

Tuesday

Priority:_____

6 _____
7 _____
8 _____
9 _____
10 _____
11 _____
12 _____
1 _____
2 _____
3 _____
4 _____
5 _____
6 _____
7 _____
8 _____
9 _____
10 _____

Wednesday

Priority:_____

6 _____
7 _____
8 _____
9 _____
10 _____
11 _____
12 _____
1 _____
2 _____
3 _____
4 _____
5 _____
6 _____
7 _____
8 _____
9 _____
10 _____

Three Priorities This Week

Getting these done will make an awesome week.

☐

☐

☐

Quarterly Plan

These actions move your quarterly plan forward.

☐

☐

☐

Eat That Frog

What have you been procrastinating on?

☐

Week Starts: _____ **Week Ends:** _____ **Quarter Ends:** _____

☐ **Thursday**	☐ **Friday**	☐ **Saturday**
Priority:_____	Priority:_____	_____
6 _____	6 _____	_____
7 _____	7 _____	_____
8 _____	8 _____	_____
9 _____	9 _____	_____
10 _____	10 _____	_____
11 _____	11 _____	_____
12 _____	12 _____	_____
1 _____	1 _____	☐ **Sunday**
2 _____	2 _____	
3 _____	3 _____	_____
4 _____	4 _____	_____
5 _____	5 _____	_____
6 _____	6 _____	_____
7 _____	7 _____	_____
8 _____	8 _____	_____
9 _____	9 _____	_____
10 _____	10 _____	_____

Finding	**Funding**	**Financing**
Actions this week to find new properties: ☐	Actions this week to access credit, investors or cash: ☐	Actions this week to access private lenders or financing: ☐
Do, Delegate, Dump	**Celebrate Life**	**Centers of Influence**
Actions this week working on your business: ☐	Fun actions this week that focus on the present. ☐	Actions to develop these relationships: ☐

Accountability Call   ☐ Next Call Scheduled   ☐ Completed

Weekly Plan for Real Estate Action Takers

☐ **Monday**	☐ **Tuesday**	☐ **Wednesday**
Priority:_____	Priority:_____	Priority:_____
6 _____	6 _____	6 _____
7 _____	7 _____	7 _____
8 _____	8 _____	8 _____
9 _____	9 _____	9 _____
10 _____	10 _____	10 _____
11 _____	11 _____	11 _____
12 _____	12 _____	12 _____
1 _____	1 _____	1 _____
2 _____	2 _____	2 _____
3 _____	3 _____	3 _____
4 _____	4 _____	4 _____
5 _____	5 _____	5 _____
6 _____	6 _____	6 _____
7 _____	7 _____	7 _____
8 _____	8 _____	8 _____
9 _____	9 _____	9 _____
10 _____	10 _____	10 _____

Three Priorities This Week

Getting these done will make an awesome week.

☐

☐

☐

Quarterly Plan

These actions move your quarterly plan forward.

☐

☐

☐

Eat That Frog

What have you been procrastinating on?

☐

Week Starts: _____ **Week Ends:** _____ **Quarter Ends:** _____

☐ **Thursday**	☐ **Friday**

Thursday

Priority:_____

6 _____
7 _____
8 _____
9 _____
10 _____
11 _____
12 _____
1 _____
2 _____
3 _____
4 _____
5 _____
6 _____
7 _____
8 _____
9 _____
10 _____

Friday

Priority:_____

6 _____
7 _____
8 _____
9 _____
10 _____
11 _____
12 _____
1 _____
2 _____
3 _____
4 _____
5 _____
6 _____
7 _____
8 _____
9 _____
10 _____

☐ **Saturday**

_____
_____
_____
_____
_____
_____
_____
_____

☐ **Sunday**

_____
_____
_____
_____
_____
_____
_____
_____

Finding	**Funding**	**Financing**
Actions this week to find new properties: ☐	Actions this week to access credit, investors or cash: ☐	Actions this week to access private lenders or financing: ☐
Do, Delegate, Dump	**Celebrate Life**	**Centers of Influence**
Actions this week working on your business: ☐	Fun actions this week that focus on the present. ☐	Actions to develop these relationships: ☐

Accountability Call   ☐ Next Call Scheduled   ☐ Completed

Weekly Plan for Real Estate Action Takers

Monday
Priority:_____

6 _____
7 _____
8 _____
9 _____
10 _____
11 _____
12 _____
1 _____
2 _____
3 _____
4 _____
5 _____
6 _____
7 _____
8 _____
9 _____
10 _____

Tuesday
Priority:_____

6 _____
7 _____
8 _____
9 _____
10 _____
11 _____
12 _____
1 _____
2 _____
3 _____
4 _____
5 _____
6 _____
7 _____
8 _____
9 _____
10 _____

Wednesday
Priority:_____

6 _____
7 _____
8 _____
9 _____
10 _____
11 _____
12 _____
1 _____
2 _____
3 _____
4 _____
5 _____
6 _____
7 _____
8 _____
9 _____
10 _____

Three Priorities This Week
Getting these done will make an awesome week.

☐

☐

☐

Quarterly Plan
These actions move your quarterly plan forward.

☐

☐

☐

Eat That Frog
What have you been procrastinating on?

☐

Week Starts: _____ **Week Ends:** _____ **Quarter Ends:** _____

☐ **Thursday**	☐ **Friday**	☐ **Saturday**
Priority:_____	Priority:_____	_____
6 _____	6 _____	_____
7 _____	7 _____	_____
8 _____	8 _____	_____
9 _____	9 _____	_____
10 _____	10 _____	_____
11 _____	11 _____	_____
12 _____	12 _____	_____
1 _____	1 _____	☐ **Sunday**
2 _____	2 _____	
3 _____	3 _____	_____
4 _____	4 _____	_____
5 _____	5 _____	_____
6 _____	6 _____	_____
7 _____	7 _____	_____
8 _____	8 _____	_____
9 _____	9 _____	_____
10 _____	10 _____	_____

Finding	**Funding**	**Financing**
Actions this week to find new properties: ☐	Actions this week to access credit, investors or cash: ☐	Actions this week to access private lenders or financing: ☐
Do, Delegate, Dump	**Celebrate Life**	**Centers of Influence**
Actions this week working on your business: ☐	Fun actions this week that focus on the present. ☐	Actions to develop these relationships: ☐
Accountability Call ☐ Next Call Scheduled ☐ Completed		

Weekly Plan for Real Estate Action Takers

	Monday		Tuesday		Wednesday

Priority:_____

6 _____
7 _____
8 _____
9 _____
10 _____
11 _____
12 _____
1 _____
2 _____
3 _____
4 _____
5 _____
6 _____
7 _____
8 _____
9 _____
10 _____

Priority:_____

6 _____
7 _____
8 _____
9 _____
10 _____
11 _____
12 _____
1 _____
2 _____
3 _____
4 _____
5 _____
6 _____
7 _____
8 _____
9 _____
10 _____

Priority:_____

6 _____
7 _____
8 _____
9 _____
10 _____
11 _____
12 _____
1 _____
2 _____
3 _____
4 _____
5 _____
6 _____
7 _____
8 _____
9 _____
10 _____

Three Priorities This Week

Getting these done will make an awesome week.

☐

☐

☐

Quarterly Plan

These actions move your quarterly plan forward.

☐

☐

☐

Eat That Frog

What have you been procrastinating on?

☐

Week Starts: _____ **Week Ends:** _____ **Quarter Ends:** _____

☐ **Thursday**	☐ **Friday**	☐ **Saturday**
Priority:_____	Priority:_____	_____
6 _____	6 _____	_____
7 _____	7 _____	_____
8 _____	8 _____	_____
9 _____	9 _____	_____
10 _____	10 _____	_____
11 _____	11 _____	_____
12 _____	12 _____	_____
1 _____	1 _____	_____
2 _____	2 _____	☐ **Sunday**
3 _____	3 _____	_____
4 _____	4 _____	_____
5 _____	5 _____	_____
6 _____	6 _____	_____
7 _____	7 _____	_____
8 _____	8 _____	_____
9 _____	9 _____	_____
10 _____	10 _____	_____

Finding	**Funding**	**Financing**
Actions this week to find new properties:	Actions this week to access credit, investors or cash:	Actions this week to access private lenders or financing:
☐	☐	☐
Do, Delegate, Dump	**Celebrate Life**	**Centers of Influence**
Actions this week working on your business:	Fun actions this week that focus on the present.	Actions to develop these relationships:
☐	☐	☐

Accountability Call   ☐ Next Call Scheduled   ☐ Completed

Monday

Priority:_____

6 _____
7 _____
8 _____
9 _____
10 _____
11 _____
12 _____
1 _____
2 _____
3 _____
4 _____
5 _____
6 _____
7 _____
8 _____
9 _____
10 _____

Tuesday

Priority:_____

6 _____
7 _____
8 _____
9 _____
10 _____
11 _____
12 _____
1 _____
2 _____
3 _____
4 _____
5 _____
6 _____
7 _____
8 _____
9 _____
10 _____

Wednesday

Priority:_____

6 _____
7 _____
8 _____
9 _____
10 _____
11 _____
12 _____
1 _____
2 _____
3 _____
4 _____
5 _____
6 _____
7 _____
8 _____
9 _____
10 _____

Three Priorities This Week

Getting these done will make an awesome week.

☐

☐

☐

Quarterly Plan

These actions move your quarterly plan forward.

☐

☐

☐

Eat That Frog

What have you been procrastinating on?

☐

Week Starts: _____ **Week Ends:** _____ **Quarter Ends:** _____

☐ Thursday

Priority:_____

6 _____
7 _____
8 _____
9 _____
10 _____
11 _____
12 _____
1 _____
2 _____
3 _____
4 _____
5 _____
6 _____
7 _____
8 _____
9 _____
10 _____

☐ Friday

Priority:_____

6 _____
7 _____
8 _____
9 _____
10 _____
11 _____
12 _____
1 _____
2 _____
3 _____
4 _____
5 _____
6 _____
7 _____
8 _____
9 _____
10 _____

☐ Saturday

_____
_____
_____
_____
_____
_____
_____

☐ Sunday

_____
_____
_____
_____
_____
_____
_____

Finding	**Funding**	**Financing**
Actions this week to find new properties: ☐	Actions this week to access credit, investors or cash: ☐	Actions this week to access private lenders or financing: ☐
Do, Delegate, Dump	**Celebrate Life**	**Centers of Influence**
Actions this week working on your business: ☐	Fun actions this week that focus on the present. ☐	Actions to develop these relationships: ☐

Accountability Call   ☐ Next Call Scheduled   ☐ Completed

Weekly Plan for Real Estate Action Takers

Monday	Tuesday	Wednesday

Priority:_____ Priority:_____ Priority:_____

Monday: 6 7 8 9 10 11 12 1 2 3 4 5 6 7 8 9 10

Tuesday: 6 7 8 9 10 11 12 1 2 3 4 5 6 7 8 9 10

Wednesday: 6 7 8 9 10 11 12 1 2 3 4 5 6 7 8 9 10

Three Priorities This Week

Getting these done will make an awesome week.

☐

☐

☐

Quarterly Plan

These actions move your quarterly plan forward.

☐

☐

☐

Eat That Frog

What have you been procrastinating on?

☐

Week Starts: _____ **Week Ends:** _____ **Quarter Ends:** _____

☐ **Thursday**	☐ **Friday**	☐ **Saturday**
Priority:_____	Priority:_____	_____
6 _____	6 _____	_____
7 _____	7 _____	_____
8 _____	8 _____	_____
9 _____	9 _____	_____
10 _____	10 _____	_____
11 _____	11 _____	_____
12 _____	12 _____	_____
1 _____	1 _____	
2 _____	2 _____	☐ **Sunday**
3 _____	3 _____	_____
4 _____	4 _____	_____
5 _____	5 _____	_____
6 _____	6 _____	_____
7 _____	7 _____	_____
8 _____	8 _____	_____
9 _____	9 _____	_____
10 _____	10 _____	_____

Finding	**Funding**	**Financing**
Actions this week to find new properties: ☐	Actions this week to access credit, investors or cash: ☐	Actions this week to access private lenders or financing: ☐
Do, Delegate, Dump	**Celebrate Life**	**Centers of Influence**
Actions this week working on your business: ☐	Fun actions this week that focus on the present. ☐	Actions to develop these relationships: ☐

Accountability Call ☐ Next Call Scheduled   ☐ Completed

	Monday		**Tuesday**		**Wednesday**

Priority:_____   Priority:_____   Priority:_____

Monday	Tuesday	Wednesday
6	6	6
7	7	7
8	8	8
9	9	9
10	10	10
11	11	11
12	12	12
1	1	1
2	2	2
3	3	3
4	4	4
5	5	5
6	6	6
7	7	7
8	8	8
9	9	9
10	10	10

Three Priorities This Week

Getting these done will make an awesome week.

☐

☐

☐

Quarterly Plan

These actions move your quarterly plan forward.

☐

☐

☐

Eat That Frog

What have you been procrastinating on?

☐

Week Starts: _____ **Week Ends:** _____ **Quarter Ends:** _____

☐ **Thursday**	☐ **Friday**	☐ **Saturday**
Priority:_____	Priority:_____	_____
6 _____	6 _____	_____
7 _____	7 _____	_____
8 _____	8 _____	_____
9 _____	9 _____	_____
10 _____	10 _____	_____
11 _____	11 _____	_____
12 _____	12 _____	_____
1 _____	1 _____	
2 _____	2 _____	☐ **Sunday**
3 _____	3 _____	_____
4 _____	4 _____	_____
5 _____	5 _____	_____
6 _____	6 _____	_____
7 _____	7 _____	_____
8 _____	8 _____	_____
9 _____	9 _____	_____
10 _____	10 _____	_____

Finding	**Funding**	**Financing**
Actions this week to find new properties: ☐	Actions this week to access credit, investors or cash: ☐	Actions this week to access private lenders or financing: ☐
Do, Delegate, Dump	**Celebrate Life**	**Centers of Influence**
Actions this week working on your business: ☐	Fun actions this week that focus on the present. ☐	Actions to develop these relationships: ☐

Accountability Call　　☐ Next Call Scheduled　　☐ Completed

Weekly Plan for Real Estate Action Takers

Monday

Priority:_____

6 _____
7 _____
8 _____
9 _____
10 _____
11 _____
12 _____
1 _____
2 _____
3 _____
4 _____
5 _____
6 _____
7 _____
8 _____
9 _____
10 _____

Tuesday

Priority:_____

6 _____
7 _____
8 _____
9 _____
10 _____
11 _____
12 _____
1 _____
2 _____
3 _____
4 _____
5 _____
6 _____
7 _____
8 _____
9 _____
10 _____

Wednesday

Priority:_____

6 _____
7 _____
8 _____
9 _____
10 _____
11 _____
12 _____
1 _____
2 _____
3 _____
4 _____
5 _____
6 _____
7 _____
8 _____
9 _____
10 _____

Three Priorities This Week

Getting these done will make an awesome week.

☐

☐

☐

Quarterly Plan

These actions move your quarterly plan forward.

☐

☐

☐

Eat That Frog

What have you been procrastinating on?

☐

Week Starts: _____ **Week Ends:** _____ **Quarter Ends:** _____

☐ **Thursday**	☐ **Friday**	☐ **Saturday**
Priority:_____	Priority:_____	_____
6 _____	6 _____	_____
7 _____	7 _____	_____
8 _____	8 _____	_____
9 _____	9 _____	_____
10 _____	10 _____	_____
11 _____	11 _____	_____
12 _____	12 _____	_____
1 _____	1 _____	_____
2 _____	2 _____	☐ **Sunday**
3 _____	3 _____	_____
4 _____	4 _____	_____
5 _____	5 _____	_____
6 _____	6 _____	_____
7 _____	7 _____	_____
8 _____	8 _____	_____
9 _____	9 _____	_____
10 _____	10 _____	_____

Finding	**Funding**	**Financing**
Actions this week to find new properties: ☐	Actions this week to access credit, investors or cash: ☐	Actions this week to access private lenders or financing: ☐
Do, Delegate, Dump	**Celebrate Life**	**Centers of Influence**
Actions this week working on your business: ☐	Fun actions this week that focus on the present. ☐	Actions to develop these relationships: ☐

Accountability Call   ☐ Next Call Scheduled   ☐ Completed

Weekly Plan for Real Estate Action Takers

☐ **Monday**	☐ **Tuesday**	☐ **Wednesday**
Priority:_____	Priority:_____	Priority:_____
6	6	6
7	7	7
8	8	8
9	9	9
10	10	10
11	11	11
12	12	12
1	1	1
2	2	2
3	3	3
4	4	4
5	5	5
6	6	6
7	7	7
8	8	8
9	9	9
10	10	10

Three Priorities This Week

Getting these done will make an awesome week.

☐

☐

☐

Quarterly Plan

These actions move your quarterly plan forward.

☐

☐

☐

Eat That Frog

What have you been procrastinating on?

☐

Week Starts: _____ **Week Ends:** _____ **Quarter Ends:** _____

☐ **Thursday**	☐ **Friday**

Thursday

Priority:_____

6 _____
7 _____
8 _____
9 _____
10 _____
11 _____
12 _____
1 _____
2 _____
3 _____
4 _____
5 _____
6 _____
7 _____
8 _____
9 _____
10 _____

Friday

Priority:_____

6 _____
7 _____
8 _____
9 _____
10 _____
11 _____
12 _____
1 _____
2 _____
3 _____
4 _____
5 _____
6 _____
7 _____
8 _____
9 _____
10 _____

☐ **Saturday**

_____
_____
_____
_____
_____
_____
_____
_____

☐ **Sunday**

_____
_____
_____
_____
_____
_____
_____

Finding	**Funding**	**Financing**
Actions this week to find new properties: ☐	Actions this week to access credit, investors or cash: ☐	Actions this week to access private lenders or financing: ☐
Do, Delegate, Dump	**Celebrate Life**	**Centers of Influence**
Actions this week working on your business: ☐	Fun actions this week that focus on the present. ☐	Actions to develop these relationships: ☐

Accountability Call   ☐ Next Call Scheduled   ☐ Completed

Weekly Plan for Real Estate Action Takers

Monday	Tuesday	Wednesday
Priority:_____	Priority:_____	Priority:_____
6 _____	6 _____	6 _____
7 _____	7 _____	7 _____
8 _____	8 _____	8 _____
9 _____	9 _____	9 _____
10 _____	10 _____	10 _____
11 _____	11 _____	11 _____
12 _____	12 _____	12 _____
1 _____	1 _____	1 _____
2 _____	2 _____	2 _____
3 _____	3 _____	3 _____
4 _____	4 _____	4 _____
5 _____	5 _____	5 _____
6 _____	6 _____	6 _____
7 _____	7 _____	7 _____
8 _____	8 _____	8 _____
9 _____	9 _____	9 _____
10 _____	10 _____	10 _____

Three Priorities This Week

Getting these done will make an awesome week.

☐

☐

☐

Quarterly Plan

These actions move your quarterly plan forward.

☐

☐

☐

Eat That Frog

What have you been procrastinating on?

☐

Week Starts: _____ **Week Ends:** _____ **Quarter Ends:** _____

☐ **Thursday**	☐ **Friday**	☐ **Saturday**
Priority:_____	Priority:_____	_____
6 _____	6 _____	_____
7 _____	7 _____	_____
8 _____	8 _____	_____
9 _____	9 _____	_____
10 _____	10 _____	_____
11 _____	11 _____	_____
12 _____	12 _____	_____
1 _____	1 _____	☐ **Sunday**
2 _____	2 _____	_____
3 _____	3 _____	_____
4 _____	4 _____	_____
5 _____	5 _____	_____
6 _____	6 _____	_____
7 _____	7 _____	_____
8 _____	8 _____	_____
9 _____	9 _____	_____
10 _____	10 _____	_____

Finding	**Funding**	**Financing**
Actions this week to find new properties: ☐	Actions this week to access credit, investors or cash: ☐	Actions this week to access private lenders or financing: ☐
Do, Delegate, Dump	**Celebrate Life**	**Centers of Influence**
Actions this week working on your business: ☐	Fun actions this week that focus on the present. ☐	Actions to develop these relationships: ☐

Accountability Call	☐ Next Call Scheduled	☐ Completed

Weekly Plan for Real Estate Action Takers

	Monday		Tuesday		Wednesday

Priority:_____   Priority:_____   Priority:_____

Monday	Tuesday	Wednesday
6	6	6
7	7	7
8	8	8
9	9	9
10	10	10
11	11	11
12	12	12
1	1	1
2	2	2
3	3	3
4	4	4
5	5	5
6	6	6
7	7	7
8	8	8
9	9	9
10	10	10

Three Priorities This Week

Getting these done will make an awesome week.

☐

☐

☐

Quarterly Plan

These actions move your quarterly plan forward.

☐

☐

☐

Eat That Frog

What have you been procrastinating on?

☐

Week Starts: _____ **Week Ends:** _____ **Quarter Ends:** _____

☐ **Thursday**	☐ **Friday**	☐ **Saturday**
Priority:_____	Priority:_____	_____
6 _____	6 _____	_____
7 _____	7 _____	_____
8 _____	8 _____	_____
9 _____	9 _____	_____
10 _____	10 _____	_____
11 _____	11 _____	_____
12 _____	12 _____	_____
1 _____	1 _____	
2 _____	2 _____	☐ **Sunday**
3 _____	3 _____	_____
4 _____	4 _____	_____
5 _____	5 _____	_____
6 _____	6 _____	_____
7 _____	7 _____	_____
8 _____	8 _____	_____
9 _____	9 _____	_____
10 _____	10 _____	_____

Finding	**Funding**	**Financing**
Actions this week to find new properties: ☐	Actions this week to access credit, investors or cash: ☐	Actions this week to access private lenders or financing: ☐
Do, Delegate, Dump	**Celebrate Life**	**Centers of Influence**
Actions this week working on your business: ☐	Fun actions this week that focus on the present. ☐	Actions to develop these relationships: ☐
Accountability Call ☐ Next Call Scheduled ☐ Completed		

Weekly Plan for Real Estate Action Takers

☐ **Monday**	☐ **Tuesday**	☐ **Wednesday**
Priority:_____	Priority:_____	Priority:_____
6 _____	6 _____	6 _____
7 _____	7 _____	7 _____
8 _____	8 _____	8 _____
9 _____	9 _____	9 _____
10 _____	10 _____	10 _____
11 _____	11 _____	11 _____
12 _____	12 _____	12 _____
1 _____	1 _____	1 _____
2 _____	2 _____	2 _____
3 _____	3 _____	3 _____
4 _____	4 _____	4 _____
5 _____	5 _____	5 _____
6 _____	6 _____	6 _____
7 _____	7 _____	7 _____
8 _____	8 _____	8 _____
9 _____	9 _____	9 _____
10 _____	10 _____	10 _____

Three Priorities This Week

Getting these done will make an awesome week.

☐

☐

☐

Quarterly Plan

These actions move your quarterly plan forward.

☐

☐

☐

Eat That Frog

What have you been procrastinating on?

☐

Week Starts: _____ **Week Ends:** _____ **Quarter Ends:** _____

☐ Thursday
Priority:_____
6 _____
7 _____
8 _____
9 _____
10 _____
11 _____
12 _____
1 _____
2 _____
3 _____
4 _____
5 _____
6 _____
7 _____
8 _____
9 _____
10 _____

☐ Friday
Priority:_____
6 _____
7 _____
8 _____
9 _____
10 _____
11 _____
12 _____
1 _____
2 _____
3 _____
4 _____
5 _____
6 _____
7 _____
8 _____
9 _____
10 _____

☐ Saturday
_____
_____
_____
_____
_____
_____
_____

☐ Sunday
_____
_____
_____
_____
_____
_____
_____

Finding	**Funding**	**Financing**
Actions this week to find new properties: ☐	Actions this week to access credit, investors or cash: ☐	Actions this week to access private lenders or financing: ☐
Do, Delegate, Dump	**Celebrate Life**	**Centers of Influence**
Actions this week working on your business: ☐	Fun actions this week that focus on the present. ☐	Actions to develop these relationships: ☐

Accountability Call   ☐ Next Call Scheduled   ☐ Completed

Weekly Plan for Real Estate Action Takers

☐ **Monday**	☐ **Tuesday**	☐ **Wednesday**
Priority:_____	Priority:_____	Priority:_____
6 _____	6 _____	6 _____
7 _____	7 _____	7 _____
8 _____	8 _____	8 _____
9 _____	9 _____	9 _____
10 _____	10 _____	10 _____
11 _____	11 _____	11 _____
12 _____	12 _____	12 _____
1 _____	1 _____	1 _____
2 _____	2 _____	2 _____
3 _____	3 _____	3 _____
4 _____	4 _____	4 _____
5 _____	5 _____	5 _____
6 _____	6 _____	6 _____
7 _____	7 _____	7 _____
8 _____	8 _____	8 _____
9 _____	9 _____	9 _____
10 _____	10 _____	10 _____

Three Priorities This Week

Getting these done will make an awesome week.

☐

☐

☐

Quarterly Plan

These actions move your quarterly plan forward.

☐

☐

☐

Eat That Frog

What have you been procrastinating on?

☐

Week Starts: _____ **Week Ends:** _____ **Quarter Ends:** _____

☐ **Thursday**	☐ **Friday**	☐ **Saturday**
Priority:_____	Priority:_____	_____
6 _____	6 _____	_____
7 _____	7 _____	_____
8 _____	8 _____	_____
9 _____	9 _____	_____
10 _____	10 _____	_____
11 _____	11 _____	_____
12 _____	12 _____	_____
1 _____	1 _____	_____
2 _____	2 _____	☐ **Sunday**
3 _____	3 _____	_____
4 _____	4 _____	_____
5 _____	5 _____	_____
6 _____	6 _____	_____
7 _____	7 _____	_____
8 _____	8 _____	_____
9 _____	9 _____	_____
10 _____	10 _____	_____

Finding	**Funding**	**Financing**
Actions this week to find new properties: ☐	Actions this week to access credit, investors or cash: ☐	Actions this week to access private lenders or financing: ☐
Do, Delegate, Dump	**Celebrate Life**	**Centers of Influence**
Actions this week working on your business: ☐	Fun actions this week that focus on the present. ☐	Actions to develop these relationships: ☐

Accountability Call   ☐ Next Call Scheduled   ☐ Completed

Weekly Plan for Real Estate Action Takers

Monday	Tuesday	Wednesday
Priority:_____	Priority:_____	Priority:_____
6 _____	6 _____	6 _____
7 _____	7 _____	7 _____
8 _____	8 _____	8 _____
9 _____	9 _____	9 _____
10 _____	10 _____	10 _____
11 _____	11 _____	11 _____
12 _____	12 _____	12 _____
1 _____	1 _____	1 _____
2 _____	2 _____	2 _____
3 _____	3 _____	3 _____
4 _____	4 _____	4 _____
5 _____	5 _____	5 _____
6 _____	6 _____	6 _____
7 _____	7 _____	7 _____
8 _____	8 _____	8 _____
9 _____	9 _____	9 _____
10 _____	10 _____	10 _____

Three Priorities This Week

Getting these done will make an awesome week.

☐

☐

☐

Quarterly Plan

These actions move your quarterly plan forward.

☐

☐

☐

Eat That Frog

What have you been procrastinating on?

☐

Week Starts: _____ Week Ends: _____ Quarter Ends: _____

☐ **Thursday**	☐ **Friday**	☐ **Saturday**
Priority:_____	Priority:_____	
6 _____	6 _____	_____
7 _____	7 _____	_____
8 _____	8 _____	_____
9 _____	9 _____	_____
10 _____	10 _____	_____
11 _____	11 _____	_____
12 _____	12 _____	_____
1 _____	1 _____	**☐ Sunday**
2 _____	2 _____	_____
3 _____	3 _____	_____
4 _____	4 _____	_____
5 _____	5 _____	_____
6 _____	6 _____	_____
7 _____	7 _____	_____
8 _____	8 _____	_____
9 _____	9 _____	_____
10 _____	10 _____	_____

Finding	**Funding**	**Financing**
Actions this week to find new properties: ☐	Actions this week to access credit, investors or cash: ☐	Actions this week to access private lenders or financing: ☐
Do, Delegate, Dump	**Celebrate Life**	**Centers of Influence**
Actions this week working on your business: ☐	Fun actions this week that focus on the present. ☐	Actions to develop these relationships: ☐

Accountability Call   ☐ Next Call Scheduled   ☐ Completed

Weekly Plan for Real Estate Action Takers

	Monday		Tuesday		Wednesday

Priority:_____ (Monday)
Priority:_____ (Tuesday)
Priority:_____ (Wednesday)

Monday:
6 _____
7 _____
8 _____
9 _____
10 _____
11 _____
12 _____
1 _____
2 _____
3 _____
4 _____
5 _____
6 _____
7 _____
8 _____
9 _____
10 _____

Tuesday:
6 _____
7 _____
8 _____
9 _____
10 _____
11 _____
12 _____
1 _____
2 _____
3 _____
4 _____
5 _____
6 _____
7 _____
8 _____
9 _____
10 _____

Wednesday:
6 _____
7 _____
8 _____
9 _____
10 _____
11 _____
12 _____
1 _____
2 _____
3 _____
4 _____
5 _____
6 _____
7 _____
8 _____
9 _____
10 _____

Three Priorities This Week

Getting these done will make an awesome week.

☐

☐

☐

Quarterly Plan

These actions move your quarterly plan forward.

☐

☐

☐

Eat That Frog

What have you been procrastinating on?

☐

Week Starts: _____ Week Ends: _____ Quarter Ends: _____

☐ **Thursday**	☐ **Friday**	☐ **Saturday**
Priority:_____	Priority:_____	
6 _____	6 _____	_____
7 _____	7 _____	_____
8 _____	8 _____	_____
9 _____	9 _____	_____
10 _____	10 _____	_____
11 _____	11 _____	_____
12 _____	12 _____	_____
1 _____	1 _____	

☐ **Sunday**

Thursday	Friday	Sunday
2 _____	2 _____	_____
3 _____	3 _____	_____
4 _____	4 _____	_____
5 _____	5 _____	_____
6 _____	6 _____	_____
7 _____	7 _____	_____
8 _____	8 _____	_____
9 _____	9 _____	_____
10 _____	10 _____	_____

Finding	**Funding**	**Financing**
Actions this week to find new properties:	Actions this week to access credit, investors or cash:	Actions this week to access private lenders or financing:
☐	☐	☐
Do, Delegate, Dump	**Celebrate Life**	**Centers of Influence**
Actions this week working on your business:	Fun actions this week that focus on the present.	Actions to develop these relationships:
☐	☐	☐

Accountability Call   ☐ Next Call Scheduled   ☐ Completed

Weekly Plan for Real Estate Action Takers

Monday	Tuesday	Wednesday

Priority:_____ Priority:_____ Priority:_____

Monday	Tuesday	Wednesday
6	6	6
7	7	7
8	8	8
9	9	9
10	10	10
11	11	11
12	12	12
1	1	1
2	2	2
3	3	3
4	4	4
5	5	5
6	6	6
7	7	7
8	8	8
9	9	9
10	10	10

Three Priorities This Week

Getting these done will make an awesome week.

☐

☐

☐

Quarterly Plan

These actions move your quarterly plan forward.

☐

☐

☐

Eat That Frog

What have you been procrastinating on?

☐

Week Starts: _____ **Week Ends:** _____ **Quarter Ends:** _____

Thursday	Friday	Saturday
Priority:_____	Priority:_____	
6 _____	6 _____	_____
7 _____	7 _____	_____
8 _____	8 _____	_____
9 _____	9 _____	_____
10 _____	10 _____	_____
11 _____	11 _____	_____
12 _____	12 _____	_____
1 _____	1 _____	
2 _____	2 _____	**Sunday**
3 _____	3 _____	
4 _____	4 _____	_____
5 _____	5 _____	_____
6 _____	6 _____	_____
7 _____	7 _____	_____
8 _____	8 _____	_____
9 _____	9 _____	_____
10 _____	10 _____	_____

Finding	Funding	Financing
Actions this week to find new properties: ☐	Actions this week to access credit, investors or cash: ☐	Actions this week to access private lenders or financing: ☐
Do, Delegate, Dump	**Celebrate Life**	**Centers of Influence**
Actions this week working on your business: ☐	Fun actions this week that focus on the present. ☐	Actions to develop these relationships: ☐

Accountability Call   ☐ Next Call Scheduled   ☐ Completed

Weekly Plan for Real Estate Action Takers

Monday

Priority:_____

6 _____
7 _____
8 _____
9 _____
10 _____
11 _____
12 _____
1 _____
2 _____
3 _____
4 _____
5 _____
6 _____
7 _____
8 _____
9 _____
10 _____

Tuesday

Priority:_____

6 _____
7 _____
8 _____
9 _____
10 _____
11 _____
12 _____
1 _____
2 _____
3 _____
4 _____
5 _____
6 _____
7 _____
8 _____
9 _____
10 _____

Wednesday

Priority:_____

6 _____
7 _____
8 _____
9 _____
10 _____
11 _____
12 _____
1 _____
2 _____
3 _____
4 _____
5 _____
6 _____
7 _____
8 _____
9 _____
10 _____

Three Priorities This Week

Getting these done will make an awesome week.

☐

☐

☐

Quarterly Plan

These actions move your quarterly plan forward.

☐

☐

☐

Eat That Frog

What have you been procrastinating on?

☐

Week Starts: _____ Week Ends: _____ Quarter Ends: _____

☐ **Thursday**	☐ **Friday**	☐ **Saturday**
Priority:_____	Priority:_____	_____
6 _____	6 _____	_____
7 _____	7 _____	_____
8 _____	8 _____	_____
9 _____	9 _____	_____
10 _____	10 _____	_____
11 _____	11 _____	_____
12 _____	12 _____	_____
1 _____	1 _____	**☐ Sunday**
2 _____	2 _____	_____
3 _____	3 _____	_____
4 _____	4 _____	_____
5 _____	5 _____	_____
6 _____	6 _____	_____
7 _____	7 _____	_____
8 _____	8 _____	_____
9 _____	9 _____	_____
10 _____	10 _____	_____

Finding	**Funding**	**Financing**
Actions this week to find new properties: ☐	Actions this week to access credit, investors or cash: ☐	Actions this week to access private lenders or financing: ☐
Do, Delegate, Dump	**Celebrate Life**	**Centers of Influence**
Actions this week working on your business: ☐	Fun actions this week that focus on the present. ☐	Actions to develop these relationships: ☐

Accountability Call   ☐ Next Call Scheduled   ☐ Completed

Weekly Plan for Real Estate Action Takers

Monday	Tuesday	Wednesday
Priority:_____	Priority:_____	Priority:_____
6 _____	6 _____	6 _____
7 _____	7 _____	7 _____
8 _____	8 _____	8 _____
9 _____	9 _____	9 _____
10 _____	10 _____	10 _____
11 _____	11 _____	11 _____
12 _____	12 _____	12 _____
1 _____	1 _____	1 _____
2 _____	2 _____	2 _____
3 _____	3 _____	3 _____
4 _____	4 _____	4 _____
5 _____	5 _____	5 _____
6 _____	6 _____	6 _____
7 _____	7 _____	7 _____
8 _____	8 _____	8 _____
9 _____	9 _____	9 _____
10 _____	10 _____	10 _____

Three Priorities This Week

Getting these done will make an awesome week.

☐

☐

☐

Quarterly Plan

These actions move your quarterly plan forward.

☐

☐

☐

Eat That Frog

What have you been procrastinating on?

☐

Week Starts: _____ **Week Ends:** _____ **Quarter Ends:** _____

☐ **Thursday**	☐ **Friday**	☐ **Saturday**
Priority:_____	Priority:_____	_____
6 _____	6 _____	_____
7 _____	7 _____	_____
8 _____	8 _____	_____
9 _____	9 _____	_____
10 _____	10 _____	_____
11 _____	11 _____	_____
12 _____	12 _____	_____
1 _____	1 _____	
2 _____	2 _____	☐ **Sunday**
3 _____	3 _____	_____
4 _____	4 _____	_____
5 _____	5 _____	_____
6 _____	6 _____	_____
7 _____	7 _____	_____
8 _____	8 _____	_____
9 _____	9 _____	_____
10 _____	10 _____	_____

Finding	**Funding**	**Financing**
Actions this week to find new properties: ☐	Actions this week to access credit, investors or cash: ☐	Actions this week to access private lenders or financing: ☐
Do, Delegate, Dump	**Celebrate Life**	**Centers of Influence**
Actions this week working on your business: ☐	Fun actions this week that focus on the present. ☐	Actions to develop these relationships: ☐

Accountability Call   ☐ Next Call Scheduled   ☐ Completed

Weekly Plan for Real Estate Action Takers

☐ **Monday**	☐ **Tuesday**	☐ **Wednesday**
Priority:_____	Priority:_____	Priority:_____
6 _____	6 _____	6 _____
7 _____	7 _____	7 _____
8 _____	8 _____	8 _____
9 _____	9 _____	9 _____
10 _____	10 _____	10 _____
11 _____	11 _____	11 _____
12 _____	12 _____	12 _____
1 _____	1 _____	1 _____
2 _____	2 _____	2 _____
3 _____	3 _____	3 _____
4 _____	4 _____	4 _____
5 _____	5 _____	5 _____
6 _____	6 _____	6 _____
7 _____	7 _____	7 _____
8 _____	8 _____	8 _____
9 _____	9 _____	9 _____
10 _____	10 _____	10 _____

Three Priorities This Week

Getting these done will make an awesome week.

☐

☐

☐

Quarterly Plan

These actions move your quarterly plan forward.

☐

☐

☐

Eat That Frog

What have you been procrastinating on?

☐

Week Starts: _____ **Week Ends:** _____ **Quarter Ends:** _____

Thursday

Priority:_____

6 _____
7 _____
8 _____
9 _____
10 _____
11 _____
12 _____
1 _____
2 _____
3 _____
4 _____
5 _____
6 _____
7 _____
8 _____
9 _____
10 _____

Friday

Priority:_____

6 _____
7 _____
8 _____
9 _____
10 _____
11 _____
12 _____
1 _____
2 _____
3 _____
4 _____
5 _____
6 _____
7 _____
8 _____
9 _____
10 _____

Saturday

_____
_____
_____
_____
_____
_____
_____

Sunday

_____
_____
_____
_____
_____
_____
_____

Finding	**Funding**	**Financing**
Actions this week to find new properties: ☐	Actions this week to access credit, investors or cash: ☐	Actions this week to access private lenders or financing: ☐
Do, Delegate, Dump	**Celebrate Life**	**Centers of Influence**
Actions this week working on your business: ☐	Fun actions this week that focus on the present. ☐	Actions to develop these relationships: ☐

Accountability Call   ☐ Next Call Scheduled   ☐ Completed

Weekly Plan for Real Estate Action Takers

Monday	Tuesday	Wednesday
Priority:_____	Priority:_____	Priority:_____
6 _____	6 _____	6 _____
7 _____	7 _____	7 _____
8 _____	8 _____	8 _____
9 _____	9 _____	9 _____
10 _____	10 _____	10 _____
11 _____	11 _____	11 _____
12 _____	12 _____	12 _____
1 _____	1 _____	1 _____
2 _____	2 _____	2 _____
3 _____	3 _____	3 _____
4 _____	4 _____	4 _____
5 _____	5 _____	5 _____
6 _____	6 _____	6 _____
7 _____	7 _____	7 _____
8 _____	8 _____	8 _____
9 _____	9 _____	9 _____
10 _____	10 _____	10 _____

Three Priorities This Week

Getting these done will make an awesome week.

☐

☐

☐

Quarterly Plan

These actions move your quarterly plan forward.

☐

☐

☐

Eat That Frog

What have you been procrastinating on?

☐

Week Starts: _____ **Week Ends:** _____ **Quarter Ends:** _____

☐ Thursday

Priority:_____

6 _____
7 _____
8 _____
9 _____
10 _____
11 _____
12 _____
1 _____
2 _____
3 _____
4 _____
5 _____
6 _____
7 _____
8 _____
9 _____
10 _____

☐ Friday

Priority:_____

6 _____
7 _____
8 _____
9 _____
10 _____
11 _____
12 _____
1 _____
2 _____
3 _____
4 _____
5 _____
6 _____
7 _____
8 _____
9 _____
10 _____

☐ Saturday

_____
_____
_____
_____
_____
_____
_____

☐ Sunday

_____
_____
_____
_____
_____
_____
_____

Finding	**Funding**	**Financing**
Actions this week to find new properties: ☐	Actions this week to access credit, investors or cash: ☐	Actions this week to access private lenders or financing: ☐
Do, Delegate, Dump	**Celebrate Life**	**Centers of Influence**
Actions this week working on your business: ☐	Fun actions this week that focus on the present. ☐	Actions to develop these relationships: ☐

Accountability Call   ☐ Next Call Scheduled   ☐ Completed

Weekly Plan for Real Estate Action Takers

☐ **Monday**	☐ **Tuesday**	☐ **Wednesday**
Priority:_____	Priority:_____	Priority:_____
6 _____	6 _____	6 _____
7 _____	7 _____	7 _____
8 _____	8 _____	8 _____
9 _____	9 _____	9 _____
10 _____	10 _____	10 _____
11 _____	11 _____	11 _____
12 _____	12 _____	12 _____
1 _____	1 _____	1 _____
2 _____	2 _____	2 _____
3 _____	3 _____	3 _____
4 _____	4 _____	4 _____
5 _____	5 _____	5 _____
6 _____	6 _____	6 _____
7 _____	7 _____	7 _____
8 _____	8 _____	8 _____
9 _____	9 _____	9 _____
10 _____	10 _____	10 _____

Three Priorities This Week

Getting these done will make an awesome week.

☐

☐

☐

Quarterly Plan

These actions move your quarterly plan forward.

☐

☐

☐

Eat That Frog

What have you been procrastinating on?

☐

Week Starts: _____ Week Ends: _____ Quarter Ends: _____

[ ] **Thursday**	[ ] **Friday**	[ ] **Saturday**
Priority:_____	Priority:_____	_____
6 _____	6 _____	_____
7 _____	7 _____	_____
8 _____	8 _____	_____
9 _____	9 _____	_____
10 _____	10 _____	_____
11 _____	11 _____	_____
12 _____	12 _____	_____
1 _____	1 _____	_____
2 _____	2 _____	[ ] **Sunday**
3 _____	3 _____	_____
4 _____	4 _____	_____
5 _____	5 _____	_____
6 _____	6 _____	_____
7 _____	7 _____	_____
8 _____	8 _____	_____
9 _____	9 _____	_____
10 _____	10 _____	_____

Finding	**Funding**	**Financing**
Actions this week to find new properties: [ ]	Actions this week to access credit, investors or cash: [ ]	Actions this week to access private lenders or financing: [ ]
Do, Delegate, Dump	**Celebrate Life**	**Centers of Influence**
Actions this week working on your business: [ ]	Fun actions this week that focus on the present. [ ]	Actions to develop these relationships: [ ]

Accountability Call   [ ] Next Call Scheduled   [ ] Completed

Weekly Plan for Real Estate Action Takers

Monday	Tuesday	Wednesday
Priority:_____	Priority:_____	Priority:_____
6 _____	6 _____	6 _____
7 _____	7 _____	7 _____
8 _____	8 _____	8 _____
9 _____	9 _____	9 _____
10 _____	10 _____	10 _____
11 _____	11 _____	11 _____
12 _____	12 _____	12 _____
1 _____	1 _____	1 _____
2 _____	2 _____	2 _____
3 _____	3 _____	3 _____
4 _____	4 _____	4 _____
5 _____	5 _____	5 _____
6 _____	6 _____	6 _____
7 _____	7 _____	7 _____
8 _____	8 _____	8 _____
9 _____	9 _____	9 _____
10 _____	10 _____	10 _____

Three Priorities This Week

Getting these done will make an awesome week.

☐

☐

☐

Quarterly Plan

These actions move your quarterly plan forward.

☐

☐

☐

Eat That Frog

What have you been procrastinating on?

☐

Week Starts: _____ **Week Ends:** _____ **Quarter Ends:** _____

[ ] **Thursday**	[ ] **Friday**	[ ] **Saturday**

Priority:_____   Priority:_____

Thursday	Friday
6 _____	6 _____
7 _____	7 _____
8 _____	8 _____
9 _____	9 _____
10 _____	10 _____
11 _____	11 _____
12 _____	12 _____
1 _____	1 _____
2 _____	2 _____
3 _____	3 _____
4 _____	4 _____
5 _____	5 _____
6 _____	6 _____
7 _____	7 _____
8 _____	8 _____
9 _____	9 _____
10 _____	10 _____

[ ] **Sunday**

Finding	Funding	Financing
Actions this week to find new properties: [ ]	Actions this week to access credit, investors or cash: [ ]	Actions this week to access private lenders or financing: [ ]
Do, Delegate, Dump	**Celebrate Life**	**Centers of Influence**
Actions this week working on your business: [ ]	Fun actions this week that focus on the present. [ ]	Actions to develop these relationships: [ ]

Accountability Call   [ ] Next Call Scheduled   [ ] Completed

Weekly Plan for Real Estate Action Takers

	Monday		Tuesday		Wednesday

Priority:_____ | Priority:_____ | Priority:_____

Monday
- 6 _____
- 7 _____
- 8 _____
- 9 _____
- 10 _____
- 11 _____
- 12 _____
- 1 _____
- 2 _____
- 3 _____
- 4 _____
- 5 _____
- 6 _____
- 7 _____
- 8 _____
- 9 _____
- 10 _____

Tuesday
- 6 _____
- 7 _____
- 8 _____
- 9 _____
- 10 _____
- 11 _____
- 12 _____
- 1 _____
- 2 _____
- 3 _____
- 4 _____
- 5 _____
- 6 _____
- 7 _____
- 8 _____
- 9 _____
- 10 _____

Wednesday
- 6 _____
- 7 _____
- 8 _____
- 9 _____
- 10 _____
- 11 _____
- 12 _____
- 1 _____
- 2 _____
- 3 _____
- 4 _____
- 5 _____
- 6 _____
- 7 _____
- 8 _____
- 9 _____
- 10 _____

Three Priorities This Week

Getting these done will make an awesome week.

☐

☐

☐

Quarterly Plan

These actions move your quarterly plan forward.

☐

☐

☐

Eat That Frog

What have you been procrastinating on?

☐

Week Starts: _____ **Week Ends:** _____ **Quarter Ends:** _____

☐ Thursday

Priority: _____

6 _____
7 _____
8 _____
9 _____
10 _____
11 _____
12 _____
1 _____
2 _____
3 _____
4 _____
5 _____
6 _____
7 _____
8 _____
9 _____
10 _____

☐ Friday

Priority: _____

6 _____
7 _____
8 _____
9 _____
10 _____
11 _____
12 _____
1 _____
2 _____
3 _____
4 _____
5 _____
6 _____
7 _____
8 _____
9 _____
10 _____

☐ Saturday

_____
_____
_____
_____
_____
_____
_____

☐ Sunday

_____
_____
_____
_____
_____
_____

Finding	**Funding**	**Financing**
Actions this week to find new properties: ☐	Actions this week to access credit, investors or cash: ☐	Actions this week to access private lenders or financing: ☐
Do, Delegate, Dump	**Celebrate Life**	**Centers of Influence**
Actions this week working on your business: ☐	Fun actions this week that focus on the present. ☐	Actions to develop these relationships: ☐

Accountability Call   ☐ Next Call Scheduled   ☐ Completed

Weekly Plan for Real Estate Action Takers

Monday

Priority:_____

6 _____
7 _____
8 _____
9 _____
10 _____
11 _____
12 _____
1 _____
2 _____
3 _____
4 _____
5 _____
6 _____
7 _____
8 _____
9 _____
10 _____

Tuesday

Priority:_____

6 _____
7 _____
8 _____
9 _____
10 _____
11 _____
12 _____
1 _____
2 _____
3 _____
4 _____
5 _____
6 _____
7 _____
8 _____
9 _____
10 _____

Wednesday

Priority:_____

6 _____
7 _____
8 _____
9 _____
10 _____
11 _____
12 _____
1 _____
2 _____
3 _____
4 _____
5 _____
6 _____
7 _____
8 _____
9 _____
10 _____

Three Priorities This Week

Getting these done will make an awesome week.

☐

☐

☐

Quarterly Plan

These actions move your quarterly plan forward.

☐

☐

☐

Eat That Frog

What have you been procrastinating on?

☐

Week Starts: _____ **Week Ends:** _____ **Quarter Ends:** _____

	Thursday		**Friday**		**Saturday**

Priority:_____   Priority:_____

6 _____	6 _____	_____
7 _____	7 _____	_____
8 _____	8 _____	_____
9 _____	9 _____	_____
10 _____	10 _____	_____
11 _____	11 _____	_____
12 _____	12 _____	_____
1 _____	1 _____	

Sunday

2 _____	2 _____	_____
3 _____	3 _____	_____
4 _____	4 _____	_____
5 _____	5 _____	_____
6 _____	6 _____	_____
7 _____	7 _____	_____
8 _____	8 _____	_____
9 _____	9 _____	_____
10 _____	10 _____	_____

Finding	**Funding**	**Financing**
Actions this week to find new properties: ☐	Actions this week to access credit, investors or cash: ☐	Actions this week to access private lenders or financing: ☐
Do, Delegate, Dump	**Celebrate Life**	**Centers of Influence**
Actions this week working on your business: ☐	Fun actions this week that focus on the present. ☐	Actions to develop these relationships: ☐

Accountability Call   ☐ Next Call Scheduled   ☐ Completed

Weekly Plan for Real Estate Action Takers

Monday
Priority:_____

6 _____
7 _____
8 _____
9 _____
10 _____
11 _____
12 _____
1 _____
2 _____
3 _____
4 _____
5 _____
6 _____
7 _____
8 _____
9 _____
10 _____

Tuesday
Priority:_____

6 _____
7 _____
8 _____
9 _____
10 _____
11 _____
12 _____
1 _____
2 _____
3 _____
4 _____
5 _____
6 _____
7 _____
8 _____
9 _____
10 _____

Wednesday
Priority:_____

6 _____
7 _____
8 _____
9 _____
10 _____
11 _____
12 _____
1 _____
2 _____
3 _____
4 _____
5 _____
6 _____
7 _____
8 _____
9 _____
10 _____

Three Priorities This Week
Getting these done will make an awesome week.

☐

☐

☐

Quarterly Plan
These actions move your quarterly plan forward.

☐

☐

☐

Eat That Frog
What have you been procrastinating on?

☐

Week Starts: _____ Week Ends: _____ Quarter Ends: _____

[ ] **Thursday**	[ ] **Friday**	[ ] **Saturday**
Priority:_____	Priority:_____	_____
6 _____	6 _____	_____
7 _____	7 _____	_____
8 _____	8 _____	_____
9 _____	9 _____	_____
10 _____	10 _____	_____
11 _____	11 _____	_____
12 _____	12 _____	_____
1 _____	1 _____	
2 _____	2 _____	[ ] **Sunday**
3 _____	3 _____	_____
4 _____	4 _____	_____
5 _____	5 _____	_____
6 _____	6 _____	_____
7 _____	7 _____	_____
8 _____	8 _____	_____
9 _____	9 _____	_____
10 _____	10 _____	_____

Finding	**Funding**	**Financing**
Actions this week to find new properties: [ ]	Actions this week to access credit, investors or cash: [ ]	Actions this week to access private lenders or financing: [ ]
Do, Delegate, Dump	**Celebrate Life**	**Centers of Influence**
Actions this week working on your business: [ ]	Fun actions this week that focus on the present. [ ]	Actions to develop these relationships: [ ]

Accountability Call   [ ] Next Call Scheduled   [ ] Completed

Weekly Plan for Real Estate Action Takers

	Monday		Tuesday		Wednesday

Priority:_____   Priority:_____   Priority:_____

Monday	Tuesday	Wednesday
6	6	6
7	7	7
8	8	8
9	9	9
10	10	10
11	11	11
12	12	12
1	1	1
2	2	2
3	3	3
4	4	4
5	5	5
6	6	6
7	7	7
8	8	8
9	9	9
10	10	10

Three Priorities This Week

Getting these done will make an awesome week.

☐

☐

☐

Quarterly Plan

These actions move your quarterly plan forward.

☐

☐

☐

Eat That Frog

What have you been procrastinating on?

☐

Week Starts: _____ **Week Ends:** _____ **Quarter Ends:** _____

☐ Thursday

Priority:_____

6 _____
7 _____
8 _____
9 _____
10 _____
11 _____
12 _____
1 _____
2 _____
3 _____
4 _____
5 _____
6 _____
7 _____
8 _____
9 _____
10 _____

☐ Friday

Priority:_____

6 _____
7 _____
8 _____
9 _____
10 _____
11 _____
12 _____
1 _____
2 _____
3 _____
4 _____
5 _____
6 _____
7 _____
8 _____
9 _____
10 _____

☐ Saturday

_____
_____
_____
_____
_____
_____
_____
_____

☐ Sunday

_____
_____
_____
_____
_____
_____
_____

Finding	**Funding**	**Financing**
Actions this week to find new properties: ☐	Actions this week to access credit, investors or cash: ☐	Actions this week to access private lenders or financing: ☐
Do, Delegate, Dump	**Celebrate Life**	**Centers of Influence**
Actions this week working on your business: ☐	Fun actions this week that focus on the present. ☐	Actions to develop these relationships: ☐

Accountability Call   ☐ Next Call Scheduled   ☐ Completed

Weekly Plan for Real Estate Action Takers

☐ **Monday**	☐ **Tuesday**	☐ **Wednesday**
Priority:_____	Priority:_____	Priority:_____
6 _____	6 _____	6 _____
7 _____	7 _____	7 _____
8 _____	8 _____	8 _____
9 _____	9 _____	9 _____
10 _____	10 _____	10 _____
11 _____	11 _____	11 _____
12 _____	12 _____	12 _____
1 _____	1 _____	1 _____
2 _____	2 _____	2 _____
3 _____	3 _____	3 _____
4 _____	4 _____	4 _____
5 _____	5 _____	5 _____
6 _____	6 _____	6 _____
7 _____	7 _____	7 _____
8 _____	8 _____	8 _____
9 _____	9 _____	9 _____
10 _____	10 _____	10 _____

Three Priorities This Week

Getting these done will make an awesome week.

☐

☐

☐

Quarterly Plan

These actions move your quarterly plan forward.

☐

☐

☐

Eat That Frog

What have you been procrastinating on?

☐

Week Starts: _____ Week Ends: _____ Quarter Ends: _____

Thursday	Friday	Saturday
Priority:_____	Priority:_____	
6 _____	6 _____	_____
7 _____	7 _____	_____
8 _____	8 _____	_____
9 _____	9 _____	_____
10 _____	10 _____	_____
11 _____	11 _____	_____
12 _____	12 _____	_____
1 _____	1 _____	_____
2 _____	2 _____	**Sunday**
3 _____	3 _____	_____
4 _____	4 _____	_____
5 _____	5 _____	_____
6 _____	6 _____	_____
7 _____	7 _____	_____
8 _____	8 _____	_____
9 _____	9 _____	_____
10 _____	10 _____	_____

Finding	Funding	Financing
Actions this week to find new properties: ☐	Actions this week to access credit, investors or cash: ☐	Actions this week to access private lenders or financing: ☐
Do, Delegate, Dump	**Celebrate Life**	**Centers of Influence**
Actions this week working on your business: ☐	Fun actions this week that focus on the present. ☐	Actions to develop these relationships: ☐

Accountability Call   ☐ Next Call Scheduled   ☐ Completed

Weekly Plan for Real Estate Action Takers

[ ] Monday	[ ] Tuesday	[ ] Wednesday
Priority:_____	Priority:_____	Priority:_____
6 _____	6 _____	6 _____
7 _____	7 _____	7 _____
8 _____	8 _____	8 _____
9 _____	9 _____	9 _____
10 _____	10 _____	10 _____
11 _____	11 _____	11 _____
12 _____	12 _____	12 _____
1 _____	1 _____	1 _____
2 _____	2 _____	2 _____
3 _____	3 _____	3 _____
4 _____	4 _____	4 _____
5 _____	5 _____	5 _____
6 _____	6 _____	6 _____
7 _____	7 _____	7 _____
8 _____	8 _____	8 _____
9 _____	9 _____	9 _____
10 _____	10 _____	10 _____

Three Priorities This Week

Getting these done will make an awesome week.

[ ]

[ ]

[ ]

Quarterly Plan

These actions move your quarterly plan forward.

[ ]

[ ]

[ ]

Eat That Frog

What have you been procrastinating on?

[ ]

Week Starts: _____ **Week Ends:** _____ **Quarter Ends:** _____

☐ **Thursday**	☐ **Friday**	☐ **Saturday**
Priority:_____	Priority:_____	
6 _____	6 _____	_____
7 _____	7 _____	_____
8 _____	8 _____	_____
9 _____	9 _____	_____
10 _____	10 _____	_____
11 _____	11 _____	_____
12 _____	12 _____	_____
1 _____	1 _____	
2 _____	2 _____	☐ **Sunday**
3 _____	3 _____	_____
4 _____	4 _____	_____
5 _____	5 _____	_____
6 _____	6 _____	_____
7 _____	7 _____	_____
8 _____	8 _____	_____
9 _____	9 _____	_____
10 _____	10 _____	_____

Finding	**Funding**	**Financing**
Actions this week to find new properties: ☐	Actions this week to access credit, investors or cash: ☐	Actions this week to access private lenders or financing: ☐
Do, Delegate, Dump	**Celebrate Life**	**Centers of Influence**
Actions this week working on your business: ☐	Fun actions this week that focus on the present. ☐	Actions to develop these relationships: ☐

Accountability Call   ☐ Next Call Scheduled   ☐ Completed

Weekly Plan for Real Estate Action Takers

Monday

Priority:_____

6 _____
7 _____
8 _____
9 _____
10 _____
11 _____
12 _____
1 _____
2 _____
3 _____
4 _____
5 _____
6 _____
7 _____
8 _____
9 _____
10 _____

Tuesday

Priority:_____

6 _____
7 _____
8 _____
9 _____
10 _____
11 _____
12 _____
1 _____
2 _____
3 _____
4 _____
5 _____
6 _____
7 _____
8 _____
9 _____
10 _____

Wednesday

Priority:_____

6 _____
7 _____
8 _____
9 _____
10 _____
11 _____
12 _____
1 _____
2 _____
3 _____
4 _____
5 _____
6 _____
7 _____
8 _____
9 _____
10 _____

Three Priorities This Week

Getting these done will make an awesome week.

☐

☐

☐

Quarterly Plan

These actions move your quarterly plan forward.

☐

☐

☐

Eat That Frog

What have you been procrastinating on?

☐

Week Starts: _____　Week Ends: _____　Quarter Ends: _____

☐ **Thursday**	☐ **Friday**	☐ **Saturday**
Priority:_____	Priority:_____	
6 _____	6 _____	_____
7 _____	7 _____	_____
8 _____	8 _____	_____
9 _____	9 _____	_____
10 _____	10 _____	_____
11 _____	11 _____	_____
12 _____	12 _____	_____
1 _____	1 _____	_____
2 _____	2 _____	☐ **Sunday**
3 _____	3 _____	_____
4 _____	4 _____	_____
5 _____	5 _____	_____
6 _____	6 _____	_____
7 _____	7 _____	_____
8 _____	8 _____	_____
9 _____	9 _____	_____
10 _____	10 _____	_____

Finding	**Funding**	**Financing**
Actions this week to find new properties:　☐	Actions this week to access credit, investors or cash:　☐	Actions this week to access private lenders or financing:　☐
Do, Delegate, Dump	**Celebrate Life**	**Centers of Influence**
Actions this week working on your business:　☐	Fun actions this week that focus on the present.　☐	Actions to develop these relationships:　☐

Accountability Call　☐ Next Call Scheduled　☐ Completed

Weekly Plan for Real Estate Action Takers

Monday

Priority:_____

6 _____
7 _____
8 _____
9 _____
10 _____
11 _____
12 _____
1 _____
2 _____
3 _____
4 _____
5 _____
6 _____
7 _____
8 _____
9 _____
10 _____

Tuesday

Priority:_____

6 _____
7 _____
8 _____
9 _____
10 _____
11 _____
12 _____
1 _____
2 _____
3 _____
4 _____
5 _____
6 _____
7 _____
8 _____
9 _____
10 _____

Wednesday

Priority:_____

6 _____
7 _____
8 _____
9 _____
10 _____
11 _____
12 _____
1 _____
2 _____
3 _____
4 _____
5 _____
6 _____
7 _____
8 _____
9 _____
10 _____

Three Priorities This Week

Getting these done will make an awesome week.

☐

☐

☐

Quarterly Plan

These actions move your quarterly plan forward.

☐

☐

☐

Eat That Frog

What have you been procrastinating on?

☐

Week Starts: _____ **Week Ends:** _____ **Quarter Ends:** _____

☐ **Thursday**	☐ **Friday**	☐ **Saturday**
Priority:_____	Priority:_____	_____
6 _____	6 _____	_____
7 _____	7 _____	_____
8 _____	8 _____	_____
9 _____	9 _____	_____
10 _____	10 _____	_____
11 _____	11 _____	_____
12 _____	12 _____	_____
1 _____	1 _____	☐ **Sunday**
2 _____	2 _____	_____
3 _____	3 _____	_____
4 _____	4 _____	_____
5 _____	5 _____	_____
6 _____	6 _____	_____
7 _____	7 _____	_____
8 _____	8 _____	_____
9 _____	9 _____	_____
10 _____	10 _____	_____

Finding	**Funding**	**Financing**
Actions this week to find new properties: ☐	Actions this week to access credit, investors or cash: ☐	Actions this week to access private lenders or financing: ☐
Do, Delegate, Dump	**Celebrate Life**	**Centers of Influence**
Actions this week working on your business: ☐	Fun actions this week that focus on the present. ☐	Actions to develop these relationships: ☐

Accountability Call   ☐ Next Call Scheduled   ☐ Completed

Weekly Plan for Real Estate Action Takers

☐ **Monday**	☐ **Tuesday**	☐ **Wednesday**
Priority:_____	Priority:_____	Priority:_____
6 _____	6 _____	6 _____
7 _____	7 _____	7 _____
8 _____	8 _____	8 _____
9 _____	9 _____	9 _____
10 _____	10 _____	10 _____
11 _____	11 _____	11 _____
12 _____	12 _____	12 _____
1 _____	1 _____	1 _____
2 _____	2 _____	2 _____
3 _____	3 _____	3 _____
4 _____	4 _____	4 _____
5 _____	5 _____	5 _____
6 _____	6 _____	6 _____
7 _____	7 _____	7 _____
8 _____	8 _____	8 _____
9 _____	9 _____	9 _____
10 _____	10 _____	10 _____

Three Priorities This Week

Getting these done will make an awesome week.

☐

☐

☐

Quarterly Plan

These actions move your quarterly plan forward.

☐

☐

☐

Eat That Frog

What have you been procrastinating on?

☐

Week Starts: _____ **Week Ends:** _____ **Quarter Ends:** _____

☐ **Thursday**	☐ **Friday**	☐ **Saturday**

Priority: _____   Priority: _____

Thursday	Friday
6 _____	6 _____
7 _____	7 _____
8 _____	8 _____
9 _____	9 _____
10 _____	10 _____
11 _____	11 _____
12 _____	12 _____
1 _____	1 _____
2 _____	2 _____
3 _____	3 _____
4 _____	4 _____
5 _____	5 _____
6 _____	6 _____
7 _____	7 _____
8 _____	8 _____
9 _____	9 _____
10 _____	10 _____

☐ **Sunday**

Finding	Funding	Financing
Actions this week to find new properties: ☐	Actions this week to access credit, investors or cash: ☐	Actions this week to access private lenders or financing: ☐
Do, Delegate, Dump	**Celebrate Life**	**Centers of Influence**
Actions this week working on your business: ☐	Fun actions this week that focus on the present. ☐	Actions to develop these relationships: ☐

Accountability Call   ☐ Next Call Scheduled   ☐ Completed

Weekly Plan for Real Estate Action Takers

Monday

Priority:_____

6 _____
7 _____
8 _____
9 _____
10 _____
11 _____
12 _____
1 _____
2 _____
3 _____
4 _____
5 _____
6 _____
7 _____
8 _____
9 _____
10 _____

Tuesday

Priority:_____

6 _____
7 _____
8 _____
9 _____
10 _____
11 _____
12 _____
1 _____
2 _____
3 _____
4 _____
5 _____
6 _____
7 _____
8 _____
9 _____
10 _____

Wednesday

Priority:_____

6 _____
7 _____
8 _____
9 _____
10 _____
11 _____
12 _____
1 _____
2 _____
3 _____
4 _____
5 _____
6 _____
7 _____
8 _____
9 _____
10 _____

Three Priorities This Week

Getting these done will make an awesome week.

☐

☐

☐

Quarterly Plan

These actions move your quarterly plan forward.

☐

☐

☐

Eat That Frog

What have you been procrastinating on?

☐

Week Starts: _____ **Week Ends:** _____ **Quarter Ends:** _____

☐ **Thursday**	☐ **Friday**	☐ **Saturday**
Priority:_____	Priority:_____	
6 _____	6 _____	_____
7 _____	7 _____	_____
8 _____	8 _____	_____
9 _____	9 _____	_____
10 _____	10 _____	_____
11 _____	11 _____	_____
12 _____	12 _____	_____
1 _____	1 _____	
2 _____	2 _____	☐ **Sunday**
3 _____	3 _____	_____
4 _____	4 _____	_____
5 _____	5 _____	_____
6 _____	6 _____	_____
7 _____	7 _____	_____
8 _____	8 _____	_____
9 _____	9 _____	_____
10 _____	10 _____	_____

Finding	**Funding**	**Financing**
Actions this week to find new properties: ☐	Actions this week to access credit, investors or cash: ☐	Actions this week to access private lenders or financing: ☐
Do, Delegate, Dump	**Celebrate Life**	**Centers of Influence**
Actions this week working on your business: ☐	Fun actions this week that focus on the present. ☐	Actions to develop these relationships: ☐

Accountability Call   ☐ Next Call Scheduled   ☐ Completed

Weekly Plan for Real Estate Action Takers

☐ **Monday**	☐ **Tuesday**	☐ **Wednesday**
Priority:_____	Priority:_____	Priority:_____
6	6	6
7	7	7
8	8	8
9	9	9
10	10	10
11	11	11
12	12	12
1	1	1
2	2	2
3	3	3
4	4	4
5	5	5
6	6	6
7	7	7
8	8	8
9	9	9
10	10	10

Three Priorities This Week

Getting these done will make an awesome week.

☐

☐

☐

Quarterly Plan

These actions move your quarterly plan forward.

☐

☐

☐

Eat That Frog

What have you been procrastinating on?

☐

Week Starts: _____ **Week Ends:** _____ **Quarter Ends:** _____

Thursday
Priority:_____
6 _____
7 _____
8 _____
9 _____
10 _____
11 _____
12 _____
1 _____
2 _____
3 _____
4 _____
5 _____
6 _____
7 _____
8 _____
9 _____
10 _____

Friday
Priority:_____
6 _____
7 _____
8 _____
9 _____
10 _____
11 _____
12 _____
1 _____
2 _____
3 _____
4 _____
5 _____
6 _____
7 _____
8 _____
9 _____
10 _____

Saturday
_____
_____
_____
_____
_____
_____
_____
_____

Sunday
_____
_____
_____
_____
_____
_____
_____

Finding	Funding	Financing
Actions this week to find new properties: ☐	Actions this week to access credit, investors or cash: ☐	Actions this week to access private lenders or financing: ☐
Do, Delegate, Dump	**Celebrate Life**	**Centers of Influence**
Actions this week working on your business: ☐	Fun actions this week that focus on the present. ☐	Actions to develop these relationships: ☐

Accountability Call   ☐ Next Call Scheduled   ☐ Completed

Weekly Plan for Real Estate Action Takers

	Monday		Tuesday		Wednesday

Priority:_____   Priority:_____   Priority:_____

Monday	Tuesday	Wednesday
6 _____	6 _____	6 _____
7 _____	7 _____	7 _____
8 _____	8 _____	8 _____
9 _____	9 _____	9 _____
10 _____	10 _____	10 _____
11 _____	11 _____	11 _____
12 _____	12 _____	12 _____
1 _____	1 _____	1 _____
2 _____	2 _____	2 _____
3 _____	3 _____	3 _____
4 _____	4 _____	4 _____
5 _____	5 _____	5 _____
6 _____	6 _____	6 _____
7 _____	7 _____	7 _____
8 _____	8 _____	8 _____
9 _____	9 _____	9 _____
10 _____	10 _____	10 _____

Three Priorities This Week

Getting these done will make an awesome week.

☐

☐

☐

Quarterly Plan

These actions move your quarterly plan forward.

☐

☐

☐

Eat That Frog

What have you been procrastinating on?

☐

Week Starts: _____ **Week Ends:** _____ **Quarter Ends:** _____

☐ **Thursday**	☐ **Friday**	☐ **Saturday**
Priority:_____	Priority:_____	_____
6 _____	6 _____	_____
7 _____	7 _____	_____
8 _____	8 _____	_____
9 _____	9 _____	_____
10 _____	10 _____	_____
11 _____	11 _____	_____
12 _____	12 _____	_____
1 _____	1 _____	
2 _____	2 _____	☐ **Sunday**
3 _____	3 _____	_____
4 _____	4 _____	_____
5 _____	5 _____	_____
6 _____	6 _____	_____
7 _____	7 _____	_____
8 _____	8 _____	_____
9 _____	9 _____	_____
10 _____	10 _____	_____

Finding	**Funding**	**Financing**
Actions this week to find new properties: ☐	Actions this week to access credit, investors or cash: ☐	Actions this week to access private lenders or financing: ☐
Do, Delegate, Dump	**Celebrate Life**	**Centers of Influence**
Actions this week working on your business: ☐	Fun actions this week that focus on the present. ☐	Actions to develop these relationships: ☐

Accountability Call ☐ Next Call Scheduled   ☐ Completed

Weekly Plan for Real Estate Action Takers

☐ **Monday**	☐ **Tuesday**	☐ **Wednesday**
Priority:_____	Priority:_____	Priority:_____
6 _____	6 _____	6 _____
7 _____	7 _____	7 _____
8 _____	8 _____	8 _____
9 _____	9 _____	9 _____
10 _____	10 _____	10 _____
11 _____	11 _____	11 _____
12 _____	12 _____	12 _____
1 _____	1 _____	1 _____
2 _____	2 _____	2 _____
3 _____	3 _____	3 _____
4 _____	4 _____	4 _____
5 _____	5 _____	5 _____
6 _____	6 _____	6 _____
7 _____	7 _____	7 _____
8 _____	8 _____	8 _____
9 _____	9 _____	9 _____
10 _____	10 _____	10 _____

Three Priorities This Week

Getting these done will make an awesome week.

☐

☐

☐

Quarterly Plan

These actions move your quarterly plan forward.

☐

☐

☐

Eat That Frog

What have you been procrastinating on?

☐

Week Starts: _____ **Week Ends:** _____ **Quarter Ends:** _____

☐ **Thursday**	☐ **Friday**	☐ **Saturday**
Priority:_____	Priority:_____	_____
6 _____	6 _____	_____
7 _____	7 _____	_____
8 _____	8 _____	_____
9 _____	9 _____	_____
10 _____	10 _____	_____
11 _____	11 _____	_____
12 _____	12 _____	_____
1 _____	1 _____	
2 _____	2 _____	☐ **Sunday**
3 _____	3 _____	_____
4 _____	4 _____	_____
5 _____	5 _____	_____
6 _____	6 _____	_____
7 _____	7 _____	_____
8 _____	8 _____	_____
9 _____	9 _____	_____
10 _____	10 _____	_____

Finding	**Funding**	**Financing**
Actions this week to find new properties: ☐	Actions this week to access credit, investors or cash: ☐	Actions this week to access private lenders or financing: ☐
Do, Delegate, Dump	**Celebrate Life**	**Centers of Influence**
Actions this week working on your business: ☐	Fun actions this week that focus on the present. ☐	Actions to develop these relationships: ☐
Accountability Call　☐ Next Call Scheduled　☐ Completed		

Weekly Plan for Real Estate Action Takers

☐ **Monday**	☐ **Tuesday**	☐ **Wednesday**
Priority:_____	Priority:_____	Priority:_____
6 _____	6 _____	6 _____
7 _____	7 _____	7 _____
8 _____	8 _____	8 _____
9 _____	9 _____	9 _____
10 _____	10 _____	10 _____
11 _____	11 _____	11 _____
12 _____	12 _____	12 _____
1 _____	1 _____	1 _____
2 _____	2 _____	2 _____
3 _____	3 _____	3 _____
4 _____	4 _____	4 _____
5 _____	5 _____	5 _____
6 _____	6 _____	6 _____
7 _____	7 _____	7 _____
8 _____	8 _____	8 _____
9 _____	9 _____	9 _____
10 _____	10 _____	10 _____

Three Priorities This Week

Getting these done will make an awesome week.

☐

☐

☐

Quarterly Plan

These actions move your quarterly plan forward.

☐

☐

☐

Eat That Frog

What have you been procrastinating on?

☐

Week Starts: _____ **Week Ends:** _____ **Quarter Ends:** _____

☐ **Thursday**	☐ **Friday**	☐ **Saturday**
Priority:_____	Priority:_____	_____
6 _____	6 _____	_____
7 _____	7 _____	_____
8 _____	8 _____	_____
9 _____	9 _____	_____
10 _____	10 _____	_____
11 _____	11 _____	_____
12 _____	12 _____	_____
1 _____	1 _____	
2 _____	2 _____	☐ **Sunday**
3 _____	3 _____	_____
4 _____	4 _____	_____
5 _____	5 _____	_____
6 _____	6 _____	_____
7 _____	7 _____	_____
8 _____	8 _____	_____
9 _____	9 _____	_____
10 _____	10 _____	_____

Finding	**Funding**	**Financing**
Actions this week to find new properties: ☐	Actions this week to access credit, investors or cash: ☐	Actions this week to access private lenders or financing: ☐
Do, Delegate, Dump	**Celebrate Life**	**Centers of Influence**
Actions this week working on your business: ☐	Fun actions this week that focus on the present. ☐	Actions to develop these relationships: ☐

Accountability Call   ☐ Next Call Scheduled   ☐ Completed

Weekly Plan for Real Estate Action Takers

☐ **Monday**	☐ **Tuesday**	☐ **Wednesday**
Priority:_____	Priority:_____	Priority:_____
6	6	6
7	7	7
8	8	8
9	9	9
10	10	10
11	11	11
12	12	12
1	1	1
2	2	2
3	3	3
4	4	4
5	5	5
6	6	6
7	7	7
8	8	8
9	9	9
10	10	10

Three Priorities This Week

Getting these done will make an awesome week.

☐

☐

☐

Quarterly Plan

These actions move your quarterly plan forward.

☐

☐

☐

Eat That Frog

What have you been procrastinating on?

☐

Week Starts: _____ Week Ends: _____ Quarter Ends: _____

☐ **Thursday**	☐ **Friday**	☐ **Saturday**
Priority:_____	Priority:_____	_____
6 _____	6 _____	_____
7 _____	7 _____	_____
8 _____	8 _____	_____
9 _____	9 _____	_____
10 _____	10 _____	_____
11 _____	11 _____	_____
12 _____	12 _____	_____
1 _____	1 _____	

☐ **Sunday**
_____

Thursday continued: 2, 3, 4, 5, 6, 7, 8, 9, 10

Friday continued: 2, 3, 4, 5, 6, 7, 8, 9, 10

Sunday continued lines: _____

Finding	**Funding**	**Financing**
Actions this week to find new properties: ☐	Actions this week to access credit, investors or cash: ☐	Actions this week to access private lenders or financing: ☐
Do, Delegate, Dump	**Celebrate Life**	**Centers of Influence**
Actions this week working on your business: ☐	Fun actions this week that focus on the present. ☐	Actions to develop these relationships: ☐

Accountability Call   ☐ Next Call Scheduled   ☐ Completed

Weekly Plan for Real Estate Action Takers

☐ **Monday**	☐ **Tuesday**	☐ **Wednesday**
Priority:_____	Priority:_____	Priority:_____
6 _____	6 _____	6 _____
7 _____	7 _____	7 _____
8 _____	8 _____	8 _____
9 _____	9 _____	9 _____
10 _____	10 _____	10 _____
11 _____	11 _____	11 _____
12 _____	12 _____	12 _____
1 _____	1 _____	1 _____
2 _____	2 _____	2 _____
3 _____	3 _____	3 _____
4 _____	4 _____	4 _____
5 _____	5 _____	5 _____
6 _____	6 _____	6 _____
7 _____	7 _____	7 _____
8 _____	8 _____	8 _____
9 _____	9 _____	9 _____
10 _____	10 _____	10 _____

Three Priorities This Week

Getting these done will make an awesome week.

☐

☐

☐

Quarterly Plan

These actions move your quarterly plan forward.

☐

☐

☐

Eat That Frog

What have you been procrastinating on?

☐

Week Starts: _____ **Week Ends:** _____ **Quarter Ends:** _____

☐ **Thursday**	☐ **Friday**	☐ **Saturday**
Priority:_____	Priority:_____	_____
6 _____	6 _____	_____
7 _____	7 _____	_____
8 _____	8 _____	_____
9 _____	9 _____	_____
10 _____	10 _____	_____
11 _____	11 _____	_____
12 _____	12 _____	_____
1 _____	1 _____	
2 _____	2 _____	☐ **Sunday**
3 _____	3 _____	_____
4 _____	4 _____	_____
5 _____	5 _____	_____
6 _____	6 _____	_____
7 _____	7 _____	_____
8 _____	8 _____	_____
9 _____	9 _____	_____
10 _____	10 _____	_____

Finding	**Funding**	**Financing**
Actions this week to find new properties: ☐	Actions this week to access credit, investors or cash: ☐	Actions this week to access private lenders or financing: ☐
Do, Delegate, Dump	**Celebrate Life**	**Centers of Influence**
Actions this week working on your business: ☐	Fun actions this week that focus on the present. ☐	Actions to develop these relationships: ☐

Accountability Call   ☐ Next Call Scheduled   ☐ Completed

Weekly Plan for Real Estate Action Takers

Monday	**Tuesday**	**Wednesday**

Priority:_____   Priority:_____   Priority:_____

Monday	Tuesday	Wednesday
6	6	6
7	7	7
8	8	8
9	9	9
10	10	10
11	11	11
12	12	12
1	1	1
2	2	2
3	3	3
4	4	4
5	5	5
6	6	6
7	7	7
8	8	8
9	9	9
10	10	10

Three Priorities This Week

Getting these done will make an awesome week.

☐

☐

☐

Quarterly Plan

These actions move your quarterly plan forward.

☐

☐

☐

Eat That Frog

What have you been procrastinating on?

☐

Week Starts: _____ **Week Ends:** _____ **Quarter Ends:** _____

☐ Thursday

Priority:_____

6 _____
7 _____
8 _____
9 _____
10 _____
11 _____
12 _____
1 _____
2 _____
3 _____
4 _____
5 _____
6 _____
7 _____
8 _____
9 _____
10 _____

☐ Friday

Priority:_____

6 _____
7 _____
8 _____
9 _____
10 _____
11 _____
12 _____
1 _____
2 _____
3 _____
4 _____
5 _____
6 _____
7 _____
8 _____
9 _____
10 _____

☐ Saturday

_____
_____
_____
_____
_____
_____
_____

☐ Sunday

_____
_____
_____
_____
_____
_____
_____

Finding	**Funding**	**Financing**
Actions this week to find new properties:　☐	Actions this week to access credit, investors or cash:　☐	Actions this week to access private lenders or financing:　☐
Do, Delegate, Dump	**Celebrate Life**	**Centers of Influence**
Actions this week working on your business:　☐	Fun actions this week that focus on the present.　☐	Actions to develop these relationships:　☐

Accountability Call　　☐ Next Call Scheduled　　☐ Completed

Weekly Plan for Real Estate Action Takers

Monday	Tuesday	Wednesday
Priority:_____	Priority:_____	Priority:_____
6	6	6
7	7	7
8	8	8
9	9	9
10	10	10
11	11	11
12	12	12
1	1	1
2	2	2
3	3	3
4	4	4
5	5	5
6	6	6
7	7	7
8	8	8
9	9	9
10	10	10

Three Priorities This Week

Getting these done will make an awesome week.

☐

☐

☐

Quarterly Plan

These actions move your quarterly plan forward.

☐

☐

☐

Eat That Frog

What have you been procrastinating on?

☐

Week Starts: _____ **Week Ends:** _____ **Quarter Ends:** _____

☐ **Thursday**	☐ **Friday**	☐ **Saturday**
Priority:_____	Priority:_____	_____
6 _____	6 _____	_____
7 _____	7 _____	_____
8 _____	8 _____	_____
9 _____	9 _____	_____
10 _____	10 _____	_____
11 _____	11 _____	_____
12 _____	12 _____	_____
1 _____	1 _____	
2 _____	2 _____	☐ **Sunday**
3 _____	3 _____	_____
4 _____	4 _____	_____
5 _____	5 _____	_____
6 _____	6 _____	_____
7 _____	7 _____	_____
8 _____	8 _____	_____
9 _____	9 _____	_____
10 _____	10 _____	_____

Finding	**Funding**	**Financing**
Actions this week to find new properties: ☐	Actions this week to access credit, investors or cash: ☐	Actions this week to access private lenders or financing: ☐
Do, Delegate, Dump	**Celebrate Life**	**Centers of Influence**
Actions this week working on your business: ☐	Fun actions this week that focus on the present. ☐	Actions to develop these relationships: ☐

Accountability Call   ☐ Next Call Scheduled   ☐ Completed

CHAPTER 7

Getting Back on Track

"Big shots are only little shots who just kept shooting." ~ Christopher Morley

Focus, Focus, Focus

Distractions happen and life happens—we can have something horrible happen—go on vacation and come back to a mess. Sometimes the daily grind of doing stops us from building our business.

Just remember, success is not a straight line but it's a squiggly path that will take you back and forth in different directions. What is most important is that in general you are moving forward and getting to where you want to go.

Social media can really do a number on your confidence. Just remember that Facebook and Instagram are other people's highlight reel and does not include all the hard work that it takes to get to where they have gotten. When I ran a marathon and posted the pics at the finish line, I was elated by the support I got on Facebook. But nobody was there when I was running in -20° weather with layers of clothes, months at a time, and going through the pain in my legs as I ran 30 kilometers for the first time and hit the runners wall. Don't worry so much about what other people are doing, focus and refocus on what your goals are.

This chapter is how to get back on track.

Forgive Yourself

Sometimes we get off track from our goals and that's okay—it's important that we are able to forgive ourselves and move on. Don't be hard on yourself, whether you have completed your goal or not. It's more important that you continue to improve yourself over time. One of the things that I have learned is that you can start from day one any time you want. Sometimes you need to start from day one again, even if you've been doing something for a very long time. For example, maybe you have been working on a diet for a long time and then all of a sudden you get sidetracked by a dessert. It throws you off your game. Instead, start the process again from day one, working towards getting those numbers back to where they were before. It does not work if day one happens every day, but it is an effective strategy in order to get you back on track.

Refer Back to Your Big Why

The other thing that is really important and will help you stay on track is understanding what your big why is. If you continue to remind yourself why you are doing what you are doing, it should help you to get the goals that you are trying to achieve. Go back and review the **Big Why** activity that you did at the beginning of this journal.

Use the Mantra

If there is a saying that you can say to yourself, that you can repeat, it makes it easy for you to accept some of the challenges that happen and some of the setbacks. If you can refer to those mantras from time to time, I've found that it helps me to continue to move forward even with challenges. One of the mantras that I use is, **"If it were easy everyone would do it."** Find a mantra that you can use that you will say or have said in the past that works for you. Another one that my friend uses is, **"If you don't take a chance, you can't sing and dance."**

What Is Your Pain Point?

When I was losing weight, I'd look back at a picture of me looking unhealthily over-weight. You work harder to avoid the pain of getting back to where you were. Some ways that people can do this is reviewing your letter to yourself from the future or your vision board or twenty-year goals, whatever you did to illustrate your long-term goals. Taking the time in reviewing your long-term goals and thinking about them would be a good way of renewing the image that you have to achieve those goals.

Redo Wheel of Life

Perhaps, it's time to redo the Wheel of Life activity and see if anything has changed. Perhaps, there is a new area of your life that you need to put on and take the time to develop. This is a great activity and can be done multiple times if you feel like you're losing the action or that you need to refocus.

Associate with Others Who Continue to Achieve

You have the average income of the five people that you hang out with. I've heard the statement again and again, that this will determine your average net worth. I really do believe that this is the case, as I have experienced it myself again and again. If you know that there are certain people who have already achieved what you are looking to achieve, find out what meetings they are attending and perhaps you can attend the same meeting with them. It is always useful to have a friendly face at any meeting, as long as it is a public meeting. You want to help other people to achieve their goals and it's even better when they are on the same journey as you.

It doesn't necessarily mean you have to be a competitor, rather you have a friend who's moving in the same direction. I've often found that there is a difference between people who have set themselves up as competitors with me and others who have set themselves up as friends. We continue to help each other to grow, when we're friends, even if we are working in the same area.

Coming Up with a Bucket List of Items

Are there things that you've always wanted to do and haven't had the time or the ability to be able to do them in the past? I have found that creating a bucket list of items that you would have liked completed in your life is a really useful activity to do in order to define your long-range goals but also to see which ones that you were able to achieve.

Use a blank sheet of paper and write out your bucket list. Don't stop writing until you have written down all the items that you can think of. Aim for adding at least one hundred items to the list.

The idea is that you continue to strive and know that there are so many more goals out there for you to achieve and all you need to do is start working towards those goals. Having a large list is a challenge, when you first look at it, but over time you'll be surprised at how many items off this list can be crossed off because you have written down and focused on it.

That's the beauty of writing your goals down and using these tools.

Shiny Object Syndrome

One of the things that you must always be careful of when you are working towards your goals is being distracted by money right now. You will often find that there are different opportunities for you to continue to make money in the area of real estate investing but not necessarily focus on investing. Some of those areas can be becoming a realtor or mortgage agent or insurance broker, whatever those jobs are they can be a very lucrative income source but not necessarily a wealth generator.

You need to watch out for other shiny objects that may be opportunities to start a business but sometimes starting a business is really just owning a job. It's something that you have to be careful when you are investing in real estate. Watch for shiny objects that are coming along that seem to be good opportunities but really will suck up all of your time and prevent you from achieving all of those long-term goals they have set for yourself.

It's funny that some people decide to leave their employment only to work five times as many hours as a self-employed person. The only difference is they are accountable to themselves being self-employed but don't necessarily run the business. You need to be careful that as you are creating a real estate investment empire, that you're not owning a job, that you are creating a business. A business is something that can run without you.

Make sure that what you are doing aligns with your long-term goals and the strategies, systems, and processes that you use to help to continue to push you towards achieving those goals.

One of the things that I have done that would be considered shiny object syndrome was completing twelve flip projects in twelve months. I worked hard to get those projects completed and was able to make a lot of money but I ended up owning a job. Flip projects were great in order to create an influx of capital. I was able to use that capital in order to get into longer-term investment projects, so in the end it was short-term pain in order to gain long term, but I was able to use the funds in order to get into some projects without joint venture partners.

If I would have stayed on my original plan and used joint venture partners for those properties, I would have been able to keep all twelve of them and continue to earn income from those properties, as well as generated long-term equity gains. I would have made at least an additional million to two million in equity on all of those projects and continued to own cash flow but came from it every month. I was distracted by the shiny object of cash.

In all of the businesses that we do when you are investing in real estate, you are always struck by the shiny object. It's like a green object that is still shiny and distracts you from your goal and it's important for you to realize when you are being distracted.

Now that you are back on track, make sure that you keep the momentum going, continue with your quarterly plans, and continue with your weekly plans.

CHAPTER 8

Conclusion

FINAL THOUGHTS

Your 20-Year Goals and Achieving Them in 3 Years

You will be able to do more in your life than you ever thought possible. It has been really amazing for me to be working with a number of coaching clients as well as Durham REI members over the years and I have been able to see their success. It's an honor to be able to hear how much they have been able to achieve by using this framework. And you can do so too. Just imagine if you were able to achieve the goals that you set for twenty years in half or even a quarter of the time, imagine what you can achieve in your lifetime.

I've had people who thought they were going to need ten years to be able to quit their job and be able to do so in three years because they were committed to the process. They were able to achieve almost all their goals every quarter.

I've had other people who have been able to purchase their first property, get their first joint venture partner, or raise their first million dollars in capital. It has been amazing to see the success of these people. The tool that I am complimented on again and again is the weekly and quarterly planning tool.

You need to continue to keep the momentum going with the successes that you have already and keep going because we are only limited by our thoughts. Set big goals and consider redoing your letter to yourself and the vision board after a few years, if you have achieved a significant amount of the goals that you have already set yourself.

Learn from the adversity and the obstacles that are in front of you. Often, I find that obstacles include opportunities if you can keep pushing forward. One of the things that I am not accepting of is the answer no. No from building departments, no from banks, no from potential partners. I am somebody who will continue to go after the goals that I have set for myself. Have that mindset and you will continue to succeed.

Just remember, achieving your goals means getting out of your comfort zone. Growth means that you have to look at further development of yourself both personally and professionally. Nothing comes from doing the same thing because you will get the same results. If you want to achieve more, you need to do more and get out of your comfort zone.

No matter where you start, there is a journey that all entrepreneurs take, whether they are real estate entrepreneurs or entrepreneurs in other areas. The journey can be quite challenging and at times you feel like you are failing, but if you take the time to enjoy the journey, life becomes a lot easier. Be grateful for all the things that you have already gotten in your life and make sure to thank the people who have given you their friendship and have supported you along the way. The more you can enjoy the journey, the easier the journey becomes because it does not feel like work or challenge anymore but more like fun.

Be sure to visit www.actiontakerrealestateplanner.com in order to download some of the resources mentioned in this book, as well as getting updates for this planner and future publications.

Suggested Reading:

Duckworth, Angela. *Grit : The Power of Passion and Perseverance.* New York; London; Toronto; Sydney; New Delhi, Scribner, 2018.

Dweck, Carol. *Mindset.* London Robinson, 2017.

Goggins, David, and Lioncrest Publishing. *Can't Hurt Me : Master Your Mind and Defy the Odds.* Miejsce Nieznane, Lioncrest Publishing, Druk, 2019.

Hill, Napoleon, et al. *5 Great Books in 1: Think and Grow Rich; The Science of Getting Rich; As a Man Thinketh; The Way of Peace ;The Science of Being Well.* Global International Ltd, 2011.

Holiday, Ryan. *The Obstacle Is the Way : The Ancient Art of Turning Adversity to Advantage.* London, Profile Books, 2015.

Author Biography – Quentin D'Souza

Quentin D'Souza is a highly respected, multiple award winning Real Estate Investor in the Ontario Real Estate Investing community. He has appeared in, and has been quoted in, many different real estate publications and books.

Quentin is a trusted authority on the Durham Real Estate Market and has worked with and mentored thousands of Real Estate Investors through the Durham Real Estate Investor Club at www.DurhamREI.ca, since 2008, and the Real Estate Investors Video Training Site at www.EducationREI.ca.

Quentin is also the author of *The Property Management Toolbox: A How-To Guide for Ontario Real Estate Investors and Landlords* (www.TheOntarioLandlordToolbox. ca), which is a comprehensive guide for getting a real estate business going. He is a coauthor of *The Ultimate Wealth Strategy: Your Complete Guide to Buying, Fixing, Refinancing, and Renting Real Estate* (www.theultimatewealthstrategy.com), which shares his strategy for building a real estate portfolio.

Quentin manages a large real estate portfolio and works with other investors using joint ventures through his company, Appleridge Homes (www.AppleridgeHomes.ca).

Quentin can often be found at one of his two sons' sports events or activities. When you see him in the community, please introduce yourself.